D1204837

THE BOOK OF JOY

The Book of Joy

A Treasury of Delights in God

Sherwood Eliot Wirt

McCracken Press
New York

McCracken Press™
An imprint of Multi Media Communicators, Inc.
575 Madison Avenue, Suite 1006
New York, NY 10022

Cover design by Tim Ladwig.

Key to Scriptural References

The King James Version
The New King James Version
The New International Version
The Englishman's Greek New Testament, with Interlinear Literal Translation
Alford's Greek New Testament

Library of Congress Cataloging-in-Publication Data:
Wirt, Sherwood Eliot.
The book of joy: a treasury of delights in God / Sherwood Eliot Wirt.
p. cm.
Includes bibliographical references and index.
ISBN 1-56977-590-7: $17.95
1. Joy—Religious aspects—Christianity. I. Title.
BV4647.J68W57 1994
241'.4—dc20 94-35095
CIP

10 9 8 7 6 5 4 3 2 1

Printed in the United States of America by Berryville Graphics.

To Ruth

La reine et la joie de mon coeur

Contents

Acknowledgments

My warm thanks go to so many who have helped to make this book a reality:

To our Lord and Savior Jesus Christ for health and strength to write my twenty-fifth book to His glory.

To my wife, Ruth, for her love, discernment and unfailing support throughout.

To Jarrell McCracken, William Griffin and Bunny Graham Dienert of McCracken Press and Laura Carr and Sam Chapin of Multi Media Communicators, Inc. for encouragement and expertise in the publication process.

To former associates in the Billy Graham Evangelistic Association, including Dr. Graham himself, Roger Palms, Esther LaDow and Virginia Anderson, for many courtesies rendered.

To members of the San Diego County Christian Writers' Guild for their friendship, help and professional skill.

To the libraries of the San Diego City and County library systems, the University of San Diego, Westminster Theological Seminary, Bethel Seminary, and Point Loma Nazarene College libraries, and the Evangelical Library of London, for their assistance.

To Ernest Owen, Sandi Dolbee, Cal Samra, Evan Wirt, Pamela Moore, John McColl, Dr. Michael MacIntosh, Dale Lowrimore, and other friends and relatives who supported me in compiling this work.

To the inspired writers of Holy Scripture who made the Bible a book of joy.

And to all those persons, living and dead, whose thoughts and writings will be found in these pages. Sincere efforts to obtain permission to reproduce such writings have been made wherever possible, and acknowledgment noted. To God be the glory!

S.E.W.
Poway, California

INTRODUCTION

Joy, the subject of this book, is an extremely significant yet often neglected aspect of Christianity. It is so important that one cannot think of the true meaning of Christian living without it. In the Bible it ranks at the top. Yet today, as in centuries past, joy remains a relatively minor topic in the great debates of theology.

To begin, I invite you to join me on an expedition to uncover the unique joy that captivated the New Testament church and made its teachings spread like an unchecked forest fire over the ancient world. We need to examine this word *joy* carefully to see if it is still relevant, and to understand how it differs from words like *happiness* and *fun* even when it includes them.

These pages are also intended to enlighten believers as to the place God has provided for joy in the life of faith. They contain neither new innovations nor old heresies, much as they may seem to do so. As the author and compiler, I have no aim in view that goes beyond setting forth the Bible as the Word of God and Jesus Christ as the Way, the Truth and the Life. From the year A.D. 1 to A.D. 2000 the Gospel of salvation has made its way into the hearts of people. When set forth under the inspiration of the Holy Spirit, it still packs its old-time power. We writers try mainly to get out of God's way.

Here our principal interest is not so much in the "meat and potatoes" of the Gospel message as in the "sauces" that give flavor to the feast, and the "dessert" that crowns the banquet. These provide the joyous qualities that give to the Gospel an appeal both indispensable and irresistible.

We want to look at some Christians whose lives have been honored throughout the world, principally because they radiated joy. We will sit at the feet of other Christians who have highly entertaining ways of expressing themselves. We shall sample some joyful thoughts, joyful poetry, and joyful songs that have delighted Christians past and present.

We also want to investigate laughter in a Christian context. As we read about the humorous situations in which sincere believers sometimes find themselves, we look for reassurance that we are all cut from the same human cloth. When joy is salvaged out of tragedy, we want to learn from that. Furthermore, we want some convincing that holiness means haleness and heartiness, and not just putting on a mask of contrived solemnity—the kind that Jesus warned against.

Perhaps more than anything else, *we want to know that God has a smile on His face.*[1] Then from a more intimate standpoint, we would learn how we can obtain for ourselves the inner joy that the disciples of Jesus displayed, that David had when he wrote the Psalms, that Paul and Silas had when they sang songs in prison.

This book will not attempt to solve the joylessness of today's world. Desperate global social conditions must find their solutions elsewhere. I do not mean to imply that Christian joy has no place in *The Social Conscience of the Evangelical* (the title of an earlier volume of mine).[2] I mean simply that this is a book of joy, by joy and for joy.

Accordingly it will endeavor to show that Christ has in His grace and mercy poured out His joy into many hearts in many ways and many places, and even into mine.

---

[1]Psalm 42:5.

[2] *The Social Conscience of the Evangelical* was published in 1968 by Harper & Row and was acclaimed "Book of the Year" by *Eternity* magazine.

PART ONE

What Joy is All About

Keep company with the more cheerful sort of the godly; there is no mirth like the mirth of believers.

—Richard Baxter

ADVENTURING

Horace Bushnell, the 19th century New England preacher and theologian, is said to have leaped out of bed one night and shouted, "I have found it! I have found the Gospel."[1]

Whether or not Bushnell found it, and which museum has acquired his bed, shall be left to those who care about such things. At times I feel like sending to every soul in Christendom a fax that says, "Listen, brothers and sisters, are you enjoying yourselves? If not, you are missing the mark. Joy is the best part of the Gospel!"

What have I found? A light is flashing on the dashboard of the church bus. Its emission system needs adjusting. The Gospel chariot is spewing cheerless carbon monoxide gas into the pure air of Heaven. In other words, Jesus came bringing a message of joy to the world, and where has it gone?

The church of the late twentieth century is committing a grave error. Part of it is thinking that renewal will come with threats of doom and judgment as people head for the hills. Another part is thinking that it will come when all the churches get together. But churches, as Lord MacLeod once said, are like steel; they only come together at white heat.

When the Holy Spirit brings revival to our generation, it will not come with black clouds and premonitions of doom. Listen to the prophet Zephaniah:

The Lord your God is with you,
He is mighty to save. He will take great delight in you.
He will quiet you with his love,
He will take joy over you with singing.[2]

Revival will come when the churches of the Nineties begin laughing and singing and loving each other, and showing the world what it means to know Jesus Christ, the Lord of Glory. It will come when Christians are filled with the joy of His salvation as they wait for His soon return.

The Bible says there is a time to laugh and a time to dance. That time is now; we've had enough alarms and complainings from the world, and enough reprimands about "levity" from religious leaders of the past. This book is intended for you, to take you into the deeper meanings of the word *joy,* to open vistas of love and laughter and delight in the Lord that you never knew.

In these pages you will learn that God really wants you in Joy Country. When you get there, you will discover that while He has a judgment prepared elsewhere in a lake of fire and sulfur for the devil and his groupies, God has another lake in the mountain meadows of Joy Country with an excursion boat docked and waiting for you.

So come aboard and have fun.

It was Sunday, July 20, 1969. The newspapers said that one out of every four people on earth was glued to a television set. That, in a word, is a lot of glue. The reason? Neil Armstrong was about to become the first living creature to walk on the moon. And what a walk that was. No PED XING, no DON'T WALK, no movable sidewalk, no bike lane.

Just moon. The papers said that as his skyboot touched the moondust, Armstrong uttered those famous words: "One small step for a man, one giant leap for mankind." No mention of womankind; those were the Sixties, not the Nineties. So much for Astronaut Armstrong.

You are about to do some exploring of your own in uncharted country. No moonscape, no landscape. No launching pads or giant leaps, but there will be excitement; in fact you may even fall on your face occasionally. If you do, so what? In the Bible people were frequently falling on their faces, but the Lord just as frequently kept raising them to their feet.

What you are approaching is Joy Country. This is the real thing: unspeakable, indescribable joy, the choicest of the gifts of the Creator.

The world knows nothing about it. The world thinks that joy is a good cigar, a gorgeous outfit, a new condo, a yacht, a red convertible, a suitcase full of bills that fell off a truck, an electric fence with police dogs. People struggle and manipulate all their lives to get what they imagine will bring them some kind of joy: fame, recognition, sex, financial independence, or whatever. Last but by no means least, they strive for the illusory joy of getting even.

In view of all this, let's raise a basic question of existence: What are we really looking for? Be honest. What do we secretly want out of life more than anything else? What do we long for so badly we can almost taste it? What is it that keeps dogging us year after year until we give up chasing the rabbit, admit defeat, fold up, and fade out?

Is it really money? Is it all these other acquisitions? Ask the people who have them and see what answers you get. Jesus said, "A man's life does not consist in the abundance of his possessions."[3] As to that other objective, getting even with somebody, doing it only makes things worse. You will never, ever, get even. You don't need to. "'Revenge is mine, I will repay,' says the Lord."[4]

None of these materialistic goals is an end in itself. They are simply the means people use in an attempt to *gain* their end. Take the end out of the picture, and—POOF!

What then is the end we really want with all this gimcrackery? It is the joy itself! Joy is what we long for more than anything. Even love is something we want because it brings on joy. When joy comes, then it's all worthwhile. Of all the words in the English language, joy is one of the very greatest. It is the secret elixir, the quintessence, the absolute embodiment of ultimate human desire.

Do you know what I am talking about? Joy is the new country we are to explore together. It is the land of God's mysterious ways and magnificent surprises, the land of music and love and laughter, the land of the earliest Christians, the land of Jesus.

God, Francis Schaeffer once said, means Christianity to be fun.[5] We are out to find the fun, whether we are young or old, rich or poor, male or female. Fun for a Christian is simply one attribute of joy. Does it sound strange and even incongruous that Christianity is fun? You haven't heard anything yet. So what special equipment will we need for this junket?

Nothing except a Bible.

You probably feel like the unattached young man who applied to join a popular couples group called the Sweethearts Club. His application was turned down. It was explained to him that to accept him as a single member of the Sweethearts Club would destroy the purpose of the club.

He protested, "I don't want to destroy it, I just want to get in on it!"

A good many folks would like to get in on the joy, but find that for a variety of reasons (which we will go into) they cannot. It's certainly not always their fault. Generations of people have been misguided into thinking that joy did not exist in Christianity (but it has been there from the beginning!). And now, having written off joy as not to be found on sacred soil, they have been looking elsewhere. Pity.

Some have turned to the philosophers. Taken as a whole, the philosophers are not my idea of a very cheerful collection of characters. Many of them consider planet Earth to be a downer, a dim bulb of woe that keeps giving off noises like "Ouch!" For peace of mind, they say, one must adopt a posture of stoical resignation. Aristotle thought happiness was nothing but "a kind of contemplative speculation"[6] (perhaps like when you're sitting under a hair dryer in a beauty salon?). Marcus Aurelius, the Roman emperor, was a Stoic who wanted not joy but "tranquillity" and "equanimity." He got war instead, and an unsavory reputation for persecuting Christians. Schopenhauer said joy is just the feeling one gets when the pain has stopped.

Others have turned to psychologists. Christian psychologists hold a built-in advantage over all the others: Jesus is their point of reference, and Jesus is a Man of joy. Without Jesus in the mind and heart of the psychologist, a patient's treatment will probably be reduced to medication and counseling. Should the patient express an interest in joy—just plain, old-fashioned joy in the goodness of being alive—he may be asked to fill out a form!

Some have turned to poetry, for the poets traditionally

speak of joy in their verses. More often than not, however, they seem to be scrambling for it without finding it. Lady Caroline Keppel wrote,

Where's all the joy and mirth
Made life a heaven on earth?

And John Donne added,

All our joys are but fantastical.

Hoping to find some more positive expressions on the subject, I paid a visit to the public library and turned on the microfiche. The following book titles came up on the screen: *The Joy of Sex, The Joy of No Sex, The Joy of Staying Sober, The Joy of Snorkeling, The Joy of Running Sled Dogs, The Joy of Geraniums*, and *The Joy of Cheesecake.*

One book went in for categories, saying we must distinguish between the joy of tenderness, the joy of self-glorification, the joy of acquisition, the joy of battle, and the joy of escape from danger. Such nice distinctions made me wonder whether I should add the joy of eating peanuts . . . .

Why is it we Christians so often turn to the Bible as a last resort rather than the first? One day I turned to the Bible, and actually got out my concordance and looked up the word *joy.* Eureka! My search was ended. I had found the cave of Aladdin.

It seems that this book, known to us as the Sacred Scriptures, lists 542 references to joy, which would include *gladness* (141), *delight* (85), *pleasure* (70), *laughter* (40), *merry* (30), *happy* (27), and a host of references in the newer Bible versions to *exuberance, jubilation, merriment, rapture, bliss, elation* and other synonyms for joy. In the Psalms alone I found 105 expressions of joy. The four Gospels, the Book of Acts, and the letters of Paul, Peter and Jude proved equally fruitful. In other words, I made the incredible discovery that

THE BIBLE IS A BOOK OF JOY.

---

[1]Gerald Kennedy, *His Word Through Preaching,* New York, Harper, 1947, p. 94.

[2]Zephaniah 3:17.

[3]Luke 12:15

[4]Romans 12:19

[5]*The Complete Works of Francis A. Schaeffer,* © Crossway Books, Vol. 3, 1982, p. 355. By permission of Good News Publishers, Wheaton, IL.

[6]Aristotle, *Nicomachean Ethics,* tr. by D. P. Chase, London, Everyman Library, 1949, Book X, p. 254.

EXCAVATING

> Then felt I like some watcher of the skies
> When a new Planet swims into his ken.
>
> —John Keats

Millions of Christians past and present have experienced the sudden joy of finding the Bible has ceased to be just an ancient book, and has become to them the living, flaming Word of God. In the year 1990, while delving into the various forms of the word *joy* in Scripture, I had a dizzying sensation of something fresh gripping my thoughts. In particular, the Gospels and the Book of Acts seemed to become vehicles of divine joy which even the agony and pain of our Lord's crucifixion and His work of divine atonement did not diminish.

About that time I began writing the book *Jesus, Man of Joy,* and as I kept digging it became clear that I was on new ground. The joyful atmosphere of Palestine during the glorious early months and years of Jesus' ministry seemed altogether unique in human experience. This intimation was supported by fresh discoveries of joy in the Psalms, the Book of Isaiah, and other parts of Scripture. In due course I was led to reflect afresh on the character of the triune God, the Creator and Giver of joy.

Every minister who preaches in a pulpit Sunday after Sunday faces the contrast between the bright, cheerful spirit of the New Testament Jesus and the somber atmosphere of some of our traditional houses of worship. It is a problem that won't go away. Jesus told stories about people dancing at a party and making merry, for example, but such behavior is not always acceptable in sacred precincts. The Puritan life instinct, having lived through regimes of rank and brazen licentiousness, recoils from such dangers. The result is that something deeply embedded that flourished in early Palestinian Christianity has been discreetly covered over, and even in our time most churches are extremely slow in bringing it back to light.[1]

The young minister today is forced to ask himself, "Do I express my normal personality when I enter the pulpit, or do I abandon it for a *persona* that is holier and more appropriate?" (This is sometimes referred to as the "stained glass voice.") And even when out of the pulpit the clergyman finds himself asking, "Is this proper? Is it reverent? Should I not be conducting myself with more dignity and solemnity such as suits my sacred office?" All this anxiety of course is created not so much by what God might think of his behavior, as by what the congregation and church officers might be saying about it. The seeds of hypocrisy find fertile ground in such conditions.

The problem has been aggravated by the way the Biblical text has been handled. Some devout, erudite translators, with the noblest and most praiseworthy intentions, have on occasion (unconsciously, no doubt) done a disservice to the church. When they have come across a scene of uproarious joyfulness in the New Testament (and there are lots of them) they have toned down the enthusiasm of the original description in the Greek language. Why? I am afraid you will have to ask them. Probably the interests of the liturgy are involved. Thus instead of a lively word such as was used in the ancient Greek text, they have chosen a more decorous and proper word which they consider appropriate for worship.[2]

Example: In Luke 10:21 we are told that when the seventy evangelists Jesus had sent out returned "with joy," Jesus "exulted in the Holy Spirit." That is a key statement. Nowhere else do we find Jesus linked with joy and the Holy Spirit. But what does it mean? How did He express the joy? Now listen carefully: the Greek word for joy here is *agalliao* which suggests an exuberant transport of delight; Spurgeon even claimed it means "leaping with joy." Palestinian Jews in Bible times did in fact express their joy by dancing, clapping hands, shouting and stamping their feet—not too different from the way we act. At some time in our lives we all jump up and down in our glee, don't we? Well, that's what was going on in Luke 10.

I don't know why, but when the word *joy* is used in verbal form as *rejoice,* it loses an indefinable *je ne sais quoi* of its lilt and flair. The word simply does not do justice to the Greek text. *Rejoice* is an excellent word. I love it; I sing it; and it appears in thousands of hymns and choruses; but unfortunately it is scarcely heard at all outside of church circles. No young mother in the Nineties telephones her husband at work to say, "I'm rejoicing because Lori ate all her Cracklin' Oat Bran this morning."

Joy on the other hand has more than a strictly religious connotation. It's a magnificent word that is immensely popular wherever English is spoken. Just to hear the word is enough to make one brighten up!

My point is that the burst of joy that came from Jesus on this occasion is subdued in translation, and we are the losers.

Other examples can be supplied. The Greek word *hilaros* (hilarious) becomes *cheerful* in English translation; *chairo* (be full of joy) becomes *hail* or *farewell*. In small but subtle ways the shouts of praise and laughter, the singing and skipping and dancing and celebrating that followed in the wake of Jesus' miraculous ministry are quietly transmuted into reverent expressions of sanctimony.

This is wrong! Piety is not a wet blanket to extinguish joy. True piety *is* joy, real joy, wonderful joy. If there were joyful expressions and activities of praise and laughter in ancient Palestine, we ought to know it. Then we ought to look again at our manner of worship. Think what it would do for Christianity if the worship of God Almighty, the Holy One of Israel, became fun!

Gladys Collins of Green Mountain, North Carolina, recently wrote to a national magazine, "I am a member of a church. The area I live in is known as the Bible Belt. I believe there are more churches here than anywhere in the world. Yet when you attend a service most places, you leave depressed. I believe we should leave joyful and full of the Holy Spirit."

Jesus said He came "that my joy might be in you and that your joy may be full."[3] It was Jesus who turned on the bright sunshine of Christian hope with the promise of pure delight. When the Gospel of Luke says that Jesus was "filled with joy in the Holy Spirit," it may not sound like fun—but it was.

God in His infinite wisdom created the whole fabric of the universe, from its axles to its perimeter, for His own enjoyment. He wants us, His creatures, to find joy in it as well. But there can be no joy without love, and that love comes from God because God is love. All this God has chosen to reveal to us in His holy Word, and the Word of God attests to its own truth.

From the beginning of human history the Father's purpose has been not just to enable us to survive. Much of what Herbert Spencer wrote a hundred years ago, defending the new evolutionary hypothesis, has been blown away; and yet people still use his expression, "the survival of the fittest." It's time to blow that away, too, for it is totally inapplicable to human beings.

The Bible teaches that God created us for His own pleasure and intended us to enjoy eternal fellowship with Himself. His plan was obvious: to place us on a carefully-conditioned planet in a warm, loving, Spirit-filled environment where we could fulfill His pleasure. How? By finding the true joy of living through worshiping and loving Him and serving each other.

When sin proved our undoing and evil threatened to destroy us, He sent His Son Jesus Christ to save us from ourselves and from the Destroyer. Jesus came bringing a joyful message of Good News to the human race concerning the Kingdom of God. Many heard and received the message and found their sins forgiven, but others turned on the Son of God and crucified Him. It was a cruel, dreadful act of shame and infamy.

Yet in the Providence of God the cross on which the Prince of Life died, instead of being a symbol of death, has become the glorious emblem of new life for millions of believers. Three days after the crucifixion, Jesus Christ won an immortal victory over sin and the grave in His bodily Resurrection. He died for our sins according to the

Scriptures, and rose for our redemption on Easter Day. Later He left us for Heaven with the promise of His return and the assurance of everlasting life with Him. Hallelujah!

Now, just what is everlasting life? It is not being everlastingly muscle-bound in duties, obligations, and responsibilities. Far from it. Let's take it from the record: The Gospel of salvation in Jesus Christ is a passport to joy. Salvation is *not* religion, it is emancipation from religion. Put another way, salvation is not being kept after school in detention, it is being dismissed from school to get out on the playground!

The Bible makes it clear that the joy of this salvation can be yours. Regardless of your condition or situation at the moment, these pages are for you. They contain nothing new, but they have some old truths that may be new to you. Their purpose is to make available to your life what you always wanted to have, and what God wants you to have. Take the cup and drink deeply. It is all joy, without toxins or side effects, and there are no hangovers. Just turn the page.

---

[1]Persons interested in pursuing this fascinating subject are encouraged to subscribe to *The Joyful Noiseletter,* published by Cal Samra, founder of the "Fellowship of Merry Christians," Box 895, Portage MI 49081.

[2]John Ellington, translation consultant for the United Bible Societies, states, "The Bible is replete with examples of [humor] that must have made the original readers smile or chuckle." He admits that "humor is notoriously difficult to translate," but adds that "Many translators are reluctant to convey humor even after it has been pointed out to them." See his "Wit and Humor in the Bible" in *The Bible Translator,* United Bible Societies, 1865 Broadway, New York, Vol. 42, July, 1991.

[3]John 15:11.

IMPASSE

It was the mother of all celebrations. Thousands of Israelites stood along the shore of the Red Sea after escaping from Egypt, and watched as God delivered them from their pursuers. Floundering and drowning in Red Sea waters were the horses, chariots, and helmeted warriors of the Egyptian army that Pharaoh had ordered to overtake Moses and his people. Four hundred years of enslavement were suddenly at an end. No more brickmaking at forced labor. No more floggings, baby killings, slave driving. Free at last!

But at first the people couldn't believe it. Then shouting broke out, and a fantastic scene took place out along the shoreline. It was a surge of wild exultation and jubilation, marked by singing and waving and clapping and leaping. Fathers tossed their children in the air. The prophetess Miriam took a timbrel in her hand and led the Hebrew women in a spirited victory dance.

> Sing to the Lord, for glorious is He!
> The horse and his rider He has hurled into
> the sea.[1]

Unfortunately it didn't last. Within days the Israelites forgot their joy as they struggled across the Arabian desert, short of food and water, but long on mutterings and complaints. "Where is this Moses? What kind of deal are we getting? My feet hurt. I need water. How much farther is it? Where's all this milk and honey we were told about? And those vines with luscious grapes? I vote to go back to Egypt."

When the food ran out, the Israelites were reduced to chewing on something called manna (manna means "What is it?"). It seemed to taste almost like cardboard. This was to be their diet for forty years. When they came to the first big range of mountains, Moses took off up one of them, and the people called an emergency session. Something had to be done about their situation.

Somebody suggested having some fun. Others said, "Why not?" So they built a fire and forged themselves a golden calf like the ones they had seen in the temples of Egypt. This seemed to call for music and a party. After a while things got out of hand and the party deteriorated into an orgy. Fights broke out. Egyptian wine flowed, and things got sticky. Suddenly it wasn't fun any more, and at that point Moses showed up.[2]

Today history has repeated itself. All over America there are Christian people who were once filled with joy because of what Jesus Christ did for them. They still love Him, still call Him Lord, still go to church, still believe they are saved; yet as the years have passed they are finding themselves wandering in a desert, sick and tired of manna. Some are secretly worshiping their own golden calf. What's wrong? They are no longer delighting themselves in the Lord or being nourished on His Word. Someone or something has stolen away from them the joy of God's salvation.

I asked some friends to help me put together a few of the things Christians and others are saying about the lack of joyfulness in their lives. The variety of answers evidenced great imagination. For easier reading I have grouped them under headings:

I feel so sorry for me.

"See, you're just not aware of my situation—I mean, what I'm going through."

"I happen to have a naturally melancholic temperament. It's just the way I am."

"It's my medication. Makes me kind of ornery. Can't be helped."

"Joyful? How can I be joyful with this &!#%$@ lawsuit hanging over me?"

"I've tried everything from acupuncture to Zen and nothing works with me."

"You try living with this excruciating thing twenty-four hours a day and see how bubbly you feel."

"Man, I wouldn't wish on my worst enemy the things that have been happening to me."

I've got a chicken-livered faith.

"I still pray, but God doesn't seem to care about me; He is all booked up somewhere else."

"If there is a God, and there must be, this planet somehow managed to drop out of His computer."

"As long as life doesn't make any sense, and I've got enough sense to know that it doesn't make any sense, how do you expect me to be happy?"

"I know I'm not good enough for God. If I did pray, I wouldn't expect Him to answer me. Why should He?"

"Oh, sure, life is full of jollity. But what about suffering? Come on, answer me."

"If God would give me something to be joyful about, I might consider it."

It's the kind of people I live with.

"I'm stuck in a quarrelsome environment. There's nothing anybody can do about it."

"Teenage kids will suck every bit of joy out of you."

"What that boss of mine puts me through shouldn't happen to a dog."

"I'm out of work and watch a lot of television. You ought to see the things people do to each other. You talking joy? Yeah, sure."

"When the people closest to you let you down, that doesn't give you much leverage for feeling great."

"If you lived with my spouse, you wouldn't have any joy either."

You're talking to the wrong person.

"It's no use trying; I couldn't change from what I am, even if I wanted to."

"It's my life and I'll do what I want with it. You do your thing and let me do mine."

"I've got a grievance against a certain individual. I like it, and I'm not about to give it up. So there."

"I'm human. God understands that, even if you don't."

"I'm right. When you see that, you will be right too."

"After I achieve my goals I will do my celebrating."

"I know what I'm doing is probably wrong, but it's fun

and I'm going to keep right on doing it."

"I'm sorry, it's a habit I just can't seem to quit."

What I want is not what I get.

"If I had the kind of shape/house/job/car/health/money/children they have, I'd be joyful, too."

Just leave me alone.

"You can have your joy. I get mine out of a bottle."

"I'm not going to do anything. I'm just going to watch this."

"I'm caught in a trap and there's nothing to be done."

"This gives me the only relief I can get."

"All the world is going to hell, and you and I with it. What's there to be joyful about?"

"Nothing ever gets better. It only gets worse. Look at me!"

"I can enjoy anything as long as these pills last."

Such remarks remind me of a cowboy entertainer I heard years ago singing over the radio. He twanged away about all his dismal experiences: His horse stepped into a badger hole, someone set fire to the bunkhouse, his sweetheart dumped him, the drought ruined the range, the herd of cattle died, the foreman let him go, his bill at the ranch house was overdue, his bank had gone into receivership, his insurance was cancelled, and his dog had run away. After strumming his guitar for a moment he added, "Now I'm gettin' dandruff."

Far be it from me to downgrade these people. God loves them and so do I. You may be one of them and God surely doesn't want to lose you! I was also one of them. Like Ezekiel, I sat where they sat.[3] They are merely telling it the way it is, as they perceive it. Honesty is the first step toward resolution.

But while they may have the truth, it is not quite the whole truth. They leave out something. Their clever, wise-cracking answers are a cover for what they really want, which is a deep soul joy, the kind that makes life not only worth living, but a daily delight. Such is the goal of all human longing, yearning, and desiring.

Many feel such delight is beyond their reach, so they settle for the bottled kind, the capsule kind, the stock market or lottery kind. To offers of true joy they respond, "Leave me alone . . . you're talking to the wrong person."

Are these people Christians? If you ask them, they will give you the assurance that they are. "Well," you might reply, "if it's true, your Christianity doesn't seem to be doing you much good."

Exactly! And that is why this book was written. Thousands of self-described Christians are out there in the wilderness of Arabia with the Israelites, molding their golden calf and hoping to have a little fun as long as the pills last. The situation is at a real impasse. Let's try a different tack.

---

[1]Exodus 15:21.

[2]Exodus 32:1-20.

[3]Exekiel 3:15.

CRAGS

We are going to change the approach. Instead of asking people, "Why don't you have more joyfulness in your life?" we're going to offer them the joy! Serve it up right out of the Bible. Put it on the church menu along with coffee and brownies. Many of those people would change their tune if they thought they really could be made to feel joy from crown of head to tip of toe.

But here is the problem: The moment these Christians put a foot down in Joy Country, they encounter formidable barriers. Massive crags loom against the skyline, peaks that are obstacles to joy and that discourage millions of earnest believers. Instead of reaching the sparkling mountain meadows where enjoyment is a way of life, our people have reached an impasse. What can they do? They're stuck. So they squat at the foot of the peaks and set up damage control.

What are these ominous, menacing crags? Very simply, they are *Sin, Stress, Pain,* and *Adversity.*

There is no secret passage leading through such crags, because there are no simple ways past the roadblocks life places in front of us. You will find excellent books on coping in every bookstore but they won't help much here. The reason is that *when the objective is joy, coping is not enough.*

Let's look at that first towering summit named *Sin.* What was the purpose of our Lord's atonement on the cross, what is the whole point of salvation from sin if there is no ultimate fulfillment and delight in the Lord? I faced that dilemma years ago. My mother-in-law was a sweet little lady until she opened her Bible; then she became very stern. She glared at me over her bifocals and told me, "Sherwood, you need to be born again." I frowned back at her with some annoyance and said, "Why? So I can be like you?" When I finally opened my heart to Jesus it was not because of her well-intentioned upbraiding, but in spite of it, and because I knew the depth and warmth of her love for me. It was also because there was no music in my soul, and I kept hearing joy-filled voices on her radio that sang the melodies of salvation.

Yes, I had a record of sin. It was more than a crag, it was a Gibraltar, an Ayers Rock, an El Capitan, but I didn't realize how big it was until I crawled through the fence (as Pecos Higgins would say) and came to Christ. Walt Whitman, the 19th century American poet, once taunted Christians in his famous "Song of Myself" because he said they "lie awake in the dark and weep for their sins."[1] But if he were alive I would say to him, "Hold on, Walt. You never did get the Gospel straight." Repentance for sin is the on-ramp that leads to salvation, and salvation is the open commuter freeway to joy!

Juanita Brown was sitting in a holding cell in a San Diego jail waiting to be sentenced to three years in prison. For years she had been an embezzler, stealing thousands of dollars from her employer. She had since come to Christ and repented. A few days earlier her mother had sent her a postcard with nine words on it, taken from the Book of the Prophet Nehemiah:

> Let the joy of the Lord be your strength.[2]

I'll let Juanita tell the rest of her story: "A deputy sheriff came for me at 8:30 in the morning and escorted me to the courtroom to wait for the judge. The room was empty: there was no court clerk, no lawyer, no district attorney, no probation officer, no family. All alone! Then I thought, *'I'm not alone. The Lord told me He would never leave me.'*

"I knew I was guilty, terribly guilty, and was truly sorry about it. Many times I had been placed on probation only to violate it. Whatever they gave me, I deserved it.

"The judge poked his head in and asked where everybody was. I said I didn't know. He came and sat down beside me. 'Well, Juanita,' he said, 'I guess it's just you and me.' He looked me straight in the eyes and spoke with a voice like gravel. 'I don't know why I feel the way I do. You hold a ticket on the next bus to prison, but something tells me to let you go home today.' He cleared his throat. 'Juanita, I'm going to give you one more chance. I never want to see you in my court again; if I do, I'll double your sentence.'

"That was the first time I experienced the joy of the Lord. That 'something' could only be God!"

Juanita Brown had set her foot down in Joy Country. Today she is an instructor for Prison Fellowship at that same jail, helping men and women to plan their futures after they are released.

In the account of David and Bathsheba in the Old Testament, King David did something that few people seem willing to do today. He acknowledged his relationship with Bathsheba as a sin.[3] Then in Psalm 51 he made a full and frank confession, and prayed that God would create in him a clean heart. At the end of the confession he pleaded with his Lord, "Restore to me *the joy of your salvation.*" Please note again: It was not God's salvation that David wanted restored; it was the *joy* of it. The salvation may hold, but if the joy of it slips away, something very precious is lost. In David's case the joy came back, as many of the Psalms bear witness.

What about *stress?* It has become the popular buzz word in the Nineties to describe emotional strain, tension, and worry. In a high-tech economy like ours stress has claimed millions of victims, and there seems little likelihood of any permanent cure coming through medication. Recovery books abound on the market dealing with manic-depressive psychosis, co-dependency, enmeshment, and other current types of stress. One authority has gone so far as to say, "Our bodies don't wear out, they stress out."

Churchgoing is no insurance against stress. Many Christians whose moral lives are above reproach find themselves under great stress because of the demands of duty and responsibility. But if discharging one's duty leaves the Christian destitute of gladness of heart over what he is doing, what's the point of it? What is its purpose? And what is the reward of devotion to duty for its own sake?

More duty?

The late Ogden Nash wrote a "Kind of An Ode to Duty" from which it is worth quoting a few lines:

> O Duty...
> Thou so ubiquitous,
> And I so iniquitous.
> I seem to be the one person in the world thou
> art perpetually preaching at who or to who;
> Whatever looks like fun, there thou art stand-
> ing between me and it, calling yoo-hoo.[4]

The apostle Paul used a Greek word quite similar in meaning to *stress*. It was *thlipsis* meaning pressure. The verb form of *thlipsis* means to squeeze or press. Curiously, this is the Greek word that the Latin translators rendered *tribulor*, which in the hands of our English translators became *tribulation*. Paul had about as much pressure in his life as any human being of any age, but what did he do about it? He wrote to the Christians of Corinth, "I overabound with joy at all our tribulation."

Joy is the answer. When the heart is joyful, things look different. A smile, a grin, an easy, jocular remark can reduce pressure swiftly by letting off steam. I have always remembered a remark by a bit player named Sergeant Billis in the World War II film *South Pacific*. It seems the sergeant's plane was shot from under him by Japanese anti-aircraft fire, and he was riding his parachute down into terrain infested with enemy troops when he remarked, "Oh, so it's going to be one of those days!"

Sometimes stress is a mountain that need not be climbed; there is a way around. That is to say, we take on duties that God never intended us to assume. When Peter asked the risen Lord about a matter involving another person that did not concern him, Jesus replied, "What is that to you?"[5]

The third crag is *pain*, which in some ways is the sharpest peak of all. It may not roar like a volcano, but it does manage to shriek. Few things in life are more important than the relief of pain. Some people live with pain every day of their lives, and find it difficult to relate their experiences to joy. For me to sit by the bedside of my dear wife of forty-six years, and listen to her unconscious groans when she was dying of cancer, was not a joyful period of my life. That joy comes now from the realization that her sufferings are over, and that she is again radiant and having a wonderful time with her Lord in the realm of everlasting bliss.

Our Lord Jesus Christ spent many hours during His brief sojourn on earth, doing good and lifting human pain and misery. In the twenty centuries that followed, His compassion has inspired millions of believers. It is worth conjecturing that after He touched a person and caused the pain to cease, joy invariably followed.

People have told me that they found joy in the midst of and in spite of their pain, and I believe them. They remind me of Stephen, the first Christian martyr, who had the unbelievable experience of seeing Jesus in His heavenly glory, even as his own body was being pelted and crushed by the stones that were hurled at him.[6]

During World War II, I served as chaplain in the United States Army Air Corps, which at that time was racially segregated. I was assigned to work with black troops, and it was one of the most wonderful experiences of my life. The soldiers taught me their songs, including one that says so beautifully what I find hard to put into words. Here is the way I remember them singing it:

> Though the load be weary,
> remember you
> don't have to bear it all.
> Just ask for grace
> to keep on going
> when the teardrops fall.
> *We have the joy of this assurance:*
> The Heavenly Father will always answer prayer,
> and He knows,

Oh yes, He knows,
just
how much
we can bear.

Adversity is a fact of everyday life that includes sin, stress, pain, and a whole lot more. That word *more* covers the unfortunate mistakes, mishaps, accidents, natural calamities and other negative developments that occur in all our lives and that we can't seem to avoid. Often they have tragic consequences. For range and scope, such adversity has no limits.

For example, I am writing in the aftermath of the 1994 Los Angeles earthquake. The media have been full of descriptions of death, devastation and suffering. The magnitude of the disaster was unimaginable. People came by the thousands into temporary shelters, crying that they had no money, no food or water, no living quarters, no insurance, and nowhere to go. It seems incongruous to speak of the joy of the Heavenly Father in relation to such a deplorable situation. Even the insurance companies, which have no perceptible theology, write off an earthquake's damage as an "act of God." In the same way, the famed psychologist William James reported the reaction of a group of scientists when a quake occurred during one of their meetings. He said the unanimous opinion of the scientists was, "It expressed intention!"[7]

Jesus told His disciples that the Heavenly Father sends the rain on "the just and the unjust."[8] That's a helpful beginning. But then how do we explain His statement that those whom the Father had "given to Him" would have "the full measure of my joy within them?" The answer apparently lies in the truth that God's grace has always enabled His children to rise above adversity.[9] As Job expressed it, "The Lord gave, and the Lord hath taken away; blessed be the Name of the Lord."[10]

In the wake of the catastrophe in southern California, it is heartening to report that many people discovered joy as they began responding to the widespread need. Strangers turned to helping each other. Volunteer workers came from distant parts to help. Hundreds of thousands of tons of food, clothing, and medicines were flown and trucked into the area, much of it coming from private sources.

The joy of the Lord is always involved when His people reach out in compassion to a world of suffering. It is involved when they offer prayers of intercession. "God forbid," said Samuel to the people of Israel, "that I should sin against the Lord in ceasing to pray for you."[11] Prayer and healing and help are all a vital part of the joy in the Lord. Jesus Christ took upon Himself the sin of the world, and it is not required that we must do the same. It is instead our high privilege to share His sufferings with joy as we seek to follow in His steps. It was "the joy that was set before Him" that enabled Jesus to endure the cross.[12]

When I think of people who have found joy even when they are going through a hard time, I recall (as I probably shouldn't) the elderly lady who found herself left with only two teeth in her mouth, but determined to praise God because they "hit." At least she illustrates the fact that joy often comes not from the dire situation itself, but from the approach one takes to it. Handley C. G. Moule, the great bishop of Durham, wrote, "If joy is not rooted in the soil of suffering, it is shallow." And the Scottish Bible teacher, William Barclay, indicated the human source of the joy: "The Christian way is not a grim struggle with events and with peo-

ple; it is a radiant and sunny-hearted attitude to life."[13]

The apostle Paul lived with the threat of imprisonment, torture, and death. Unfortunate circumstances were his daily diet, yet he told the elders of the church of Ephesus when his ship stopped at Miletus that he intended to finish his course "with joy."[14] Jesus Himself said to His disciples, "No one will take your joy from you."[15] It seems so sad that we continue to *take joy from ourselves* when the Lord is offering it so freely.

At the time of the earthquake I was researching the Heidelberg Catechism, a document written in 1562 by two young German theologues, Kaspar Olevianus and Zacharias Ursinus.[16] One historian calls it "the most sweet-spirited and experiential" of the Reformation writings. As a teaching tool for young Christians, it says much about sin and redemption, and it also speaks of joy. Its opening sentence reads:

"What is your only comfort in life and in death?"

"That I, with body and soul, both in life and in death, am not my own, but belong to my faithful Savior Jesus Christ, who with His precious blood has fully satisfied for all my sins, and redeemed me from the power of the devil; and so preserves me that without the will of my Father in Heaven not a hair can fall from my head; yes, that all things must work together for my salvation. By His Holy Spirit, He also assures me of eternal life, and makes me heartily willing and ready from now on to live for Him."

This catechism is surely a great treasure of evangelical faith. In it can be found sound Biblical undergirding and spiritual guidance. It has led me to grapple afresh with the enigmatic issue of God and evil that is posed by such natural disasters as the Los Angeles earthquake. Using the catechism and a dialogue form, I have attempted to put the joy of the Lord into perspective with the reality of adversity. My subject is a fictional young father who has been victimized by the earthquake, and who (in a dream sequence) challenges the possibility of finding joy amid human anguish. In the pages that follow he asks the right questions; whether he takes joy in the answers—and whether they are correct—is for you to decide. I have given this man the name of John Swingley.

---

[1]Walt Whitman, "Song of Myself," #32, in *Leaves of Grass,* New York, Modern Library, 1921, p. 51.

[2]Nehemiah 8:10.

[3]2 Samuel 12:13.

[4]Excerpted from the poem, "Kind of An Ode to Duty," from *I'm a Stranger Here Myself,* by Ogden Nash. Copyright 1935 by Ogden Nash, it first appeared in *The Saturday Evening Post.* By permission of Little, Brown and Company.

[5]John 21:22.

[6]Cf. Acts 7:54-57.

[7]Perhaps this is the place to mention that according to press reports, the pornography industry suffered heavily in the 1994 Los Angeles earthquake.

[8]Matthew 5:45.

[9]John 17:13.

[10]Job 1:21.

[11]1 Samuel 12:12.

[12]Hebrews 12:2.

[13]William Barclay, "Letters to the Philippians, Colossians and Thessalonians," in *The Daily Study Bible,* Philadelphia, Westminster Press, 1975, p. 110.

[14]Acts 20:24.

[15]John 16:22.

[16]*The Heidelberg Catechism* is published in English by CRC Publications, 2850 Kalamazoo SE, Grand Rapids, MI 49560.

The Catechism

At 4:31 on the morning of January 17th, 1994, John Swingley, computer engineer and cost accountant, was sleeping in his home in Sherman Oaks, California, when the earthquake struck. At the first shock he and his wife and daughter evacuated their house. Once the family was safely outside, the four-year-old, Flora, began to scream for her pet hamster. John's wife, Nancy, tried to hold him back, but he raced inside to rescue it. As he was carrying the cage past his fireplace an aftershock occurred. The chimney cracked and toppled, the roof collapsed, and he was knocked unconscious by falling bricks.

While John lay hospitalized in a coma in nearby Granada Hills, he had a dream. In this dream he was standing before the massive Gate of Heaven, facing a colorfully but modestly dressed young woman seated at a white table. She was, of course, working at a computer. As nearly as John could recall later, their conversation went like this:

WOMAN: Welcome, Mr. Swingley. I am Phoebe, and your file has just come up. I see you have been a lifelong member of a Reformed Christian church in Santa Monica.

JOHN: That's right.

PHOEBE: Well, blessings on you. You are about to enter into the joy of the Lord.

J. I don't want it.

P. We expected that. Let me assure you, you'll get over it.

J. I don't want anything to do with you. I want my wife and daughter. I want to get on with my life. Who kicked off this earthquake anyway?

P. I can refer you to our seismology section if you wish.

J. Forget it. I've been reading a book on joy. This author says that joy comes from God. So where is it?

P. You'll find out.

J. I don't need to find out. My joy is with my family. What you can tell me, perhaps, is where these earthquakes and hurricanes and volcanic eruptions came from in the first place.

P. Why?

J. Yes, why? Nobody will tell me. They don't even ask the question. All the media talk about is faults and pressures and Richter scales. Oh, yes, and "the next big one." And when I ask "Why?", people shrug. They act as if it just sort of happens.

P. That's wrong. In God's universe things do not "sort of happen."

J. There you go. And so I'm dead, and I've lost my wife and daughter, and you say it didn't even happen. Well, I tell you, it did happen, and somebody did it, and I want to know who.

P. *Whom.* Your family is fine, John. So are you. If you wish, you can go in now.

J. Look, just level with me. Did God set up that earthquake? Is that what the Bible teaches? If so, was He angry with me? Or just with the earth?

P. The earthquake did not strike you, John. The falling bricks did.

J. Aren't you quibbling, for Heaven's sake?

P. Not altogether. And I wouldn't say our Heavenly Father is angry at the earth itself or any of the planets. The Earth fulfills its function very well. It wobbles a bit as it goes through its orbit, but it keeps excellent time. The Heavenly Father is quite fond of the Earth. He calls it His garden. Not only that, He has promised that someday there will be peace on Earth, and the wolf will lie down with the lamb.[1]

J. Meanwhile, what about the people who died in the earthquake? Just statistics, right?

P. You have been going to church all your life, John. You studied the catechism along with the Bible in Sunday School. You know the people on Earth have been in the shadowlands for a long time.

J. I'm not sure I know what you mean.

P. Refresh your memory. Ever since the fall and disobedience of your first parents, the human race has been corrupted. It knows what to do but doesn't do it. It knows what not to do but does it. To use the language of the Bible, it is under a curse.

J. Did God do that?

P. No. The Heavenly Father created humankind in His own image, in righteousness and holiness, so that people would glorify Him and love Him in their hearts, and live with Him in eternal joy.

J. Then why the curse? Why did He have to make such a big deal of it?

P. People broke His law, and are still breaking it. You broke it yourself. That's what provoked the response. You should know that.

J. Well, I read the papers and watch television. I know there's big trouble almost everywhere. But—

P. Yes?

J. Well, why do we have to have so much of it? I mean, violence and wars and nuclear explosions and racial prejudice and pornography and drugs and scandal and crime and pollution and now earthquakes. I would say the human race is in ghastly shape. And I think God should do something about it.

P. Are you blaming God for what people do?

J. I'm not blaming God.

P. I know. That is because you have faith.

J. Do I? I guess I do. Tell me about it.

P. Remember your catechism? Faith is a sure knowledge by which God reveals truth to you in His Word, and a heart-filled trust which the Holy Spirit works in you by the Gospel. This convinces you that God freely gives you forgiveness of sins, everlasting righteousness, and salvation. By the grace of our Lord Jesus Christ, you became a new creation, born of the Spirit.

J. Well, I'll go along with that. But you haven't answered my question. Let me put it this way. How can anybody think of God as a God of joy when His creation is such a mess?

P. His creation is not a mess.

J. Well, our world, then.

P. What about your world? Hawaii, the Paradise of the Pacific, was once a volcanic explosion. John, the only thing wrong with your world is sin, and your Heavenly Father has nothing to do with that except to forgive it.

J. That's not so. Isn't God angry? Doesn't the Bible talk about His wrath? Doesn't it say He executes judgment on the wicked? How can He go around judging people and be forgiving at the same time?

P. You know He doesn't do that. He forgives people who repent. He does it because He loves to do it, and because His Son reconciled the world to Himself at the Cross.[2]

J. How?

P. He bore your sin, lifted the curse, defeated the devil, and rose from the dead. And—He sent His Spirit into the church.

J. And stopped the earthquakes. Only He didn't.

P. That's right. And the rain still falls on the just and the unjust. Some mysteries have never been revealed to us.

J. That means you can't answer my question: How can God be angry and full of joy at the same time?

P. Once more: God's anger is not a cause, it is an effect, a response to human disobedience. God is Spirit. God is also love, and love invariably leads to joy. But joy is not an effect like wrath, it is the cause, the supreme gift of God to His creation. The universe is an expression of His joy.

J. So anger is a reflex action?

P. Yes, basically. God is grieved at the sinful condition of the human race; and just as love leads to joy, so sin results in punishment either on earth or later, unless it is dealt with at the cross while there is life.

J. Then according to you, I am here as a result of God's punishment, when all I did was try to rescue my child's hamster?

P. No. I was responding to your earlier statement. You said you thought the Heavenly Father ought to do something about the condition of human society.

J. I do.

P. Perhaps He has already done something.

J. You mean He sent the Los Angeles earthquake that killed a lot of people when they were asleep? You call that punishment?

P. I was not speaking of the earthquake. Remember that the movement of the Earth, by itself, was responsible for only part of the damage and loss of life. The things people erected on the surface of the Earth collapsed and caused a great deal of the tragedy.

J. I don't consider that a very good answer. Earthquakes have always killed people. I'm still mystified. But you said God had "done something." What?

P. I was speaking of the redemption of the world that took place two thousand years ago. There were earthquakes then, too. One of them opened the empty tomb.

J. I know about Calvary, but I don't get the connection.

P. It's in the Bible, and it's also in your catechism. By the one sacrifice of His body on the cross our Lord Jesus has redeemed you and all who love Him, has washed you from your sins in His own blood, and by His grace has justified you in His sight and made you kings and priests to God and His Father, to whom be glory and dominion forever.[3]

J. You keep going back to that. Is that the only answer you have?

P. It's the only answer there is.

J. Well, I may as well own up. I do remember the catechism—parts of it. I remember that "in all my distress and persecution, with uplifted head I look for the selfsame One who has before offered Himself for me . . . who has removed from me all curse, and . . . who shall take me, with Himself and with all His chosen ones, into Heavenly joy and glory." I don't think I got it exactly.

P. Close enough. And it seems your time is now here.

J. I feel in my heart the beginning of something strange, but don't know just—I can't describe what it is. I never felt it before. It seems I still ought to be angry and grieving, but instead I keep saying to myself, "Jesus. Jesus." I feel almost light-hearted, as if everything's going to resolve itself. It doesn't make sense, does it?

J. Come, John Swingley, blessed of the Lord. Your tour of duty is over. There is no grief or anger here. Your Heavenly Father's eye is on the sparrow, and it is also on your dear wife Nancy and on little Flora. There are things on earth that cannot be shaken by any temblor. It will all work out, and your family will be looked after until the Lord Jesus returns for His own.

J. And when will that be?

P. Who knows?

J. So where's the joy?

P. You are about to enter it.

At precisely that moment John Swingley emerged from his coma and awoke in the Granada Hills hospital to the hugs and kisses of his little daughter Flora and his wife Nancy.

---

[1]Isaiah 11:6.

[2]Cf. 2 Corinthians 5:1.

[3]Revelation 1:5-6.

Singing

> From now on I will tell you of new things, of hidden things unknown to you.
>
> —Isaiah 48:6

It is obvious that we can do nothing. God holds the solution to our problem with joy. The meadows, the crags, everything in the universe belongs to Him—except sin. Right now we are camped at base of the crags, "regrouping" and "consolidating" as it is called.

In such a situation the Christian has one great recourse: the Bible. Here the wisdom of eternity is encapsulated. While our minds may be finite and our understanding limited, we shall take this question of the origin of joy right to the Source.

Our starting point will be a passage from the Book of Job. It contains the Almighty's response after Job has wound up his long complaint about the injustice of what has happened to him. Job, it will be recalled, was a wealthy landowner who lost first his house and livelihood, then his family, and finally his own health. As Chapter 38 opens, we hear the beginning of God's response to Job.

Who is this that darkens my counsel
   with words without knowledge?
Brace yourself like a man;
   I will question you,
   and you shall answer me.

Where were you when I laid the earth's foundation?
   Tell me, if you understand.
Who marked off its dimensions? Surely you know!
   Who stretched a measuring line across it?
On what were its footings set,
   or who laid its cornerstone—
while the morning stars sang together
and all the sons of God shouted for joy?

Have you ever looked up on a starry night and wondered how all that dazzling beauty related to you? Have you ever examined the planets through a telescope or even a powerful set of binoculars? We are about to examine the true motive of God in creation. Why did He make the universe?

Look at the last two lines of the passage just quoted. Note that the "sons of God" were shouting for joy when God laid "the earth's foundation." Evidently there was joy present at the creation and it was a time for celebrating with noise—but not necessarily with a "big bang."

Note also that the stars were singing. This seems to present a problem to some Bible scholars, who have decided that the stars mentioned in the text were not really stars at all. What were they, then? The usual answer is that they were angels.

That conclusion is arrived at by speculation, because nowhere in Scripture are the stars confused with angels, and nowhere do we find a clear statement that angels ever sang (Christmas carols to the contrary notwithstanding).

What Scripture tells us plainly is that the sons of God were sons of God, and the stars were stars, and that together they were celebrating at the dawn of creation. The fact that the stars made music at that time helps to explain why they were called "morning stars." Scripture says further that the stars in their courses sang "together."[1] Were they singing in harmony or disharmony? Obviously the stars were "totally subordinate to God and under His control,"[2] for He knows each one "by name," and God is not the author of discord.

Usually stars are regarded today as shining rather than singing, but Professor Franz Delitzsch has an interesting comment about that. He says, "Joy and light are reciprocal notions, and the scale of the tones of joy is likened to the scale of light and colors."[3] So the stars give off light; light is in order to joy, and joy is in order to music. Are you with me?

God, it appears, wove harmonious music into the tapestry of His universe at creation. And why would He do that, if not in joy and for joy? Everyone knows that music and joy have a natural affinity; here the Bible confirms it. The prophet Zephaniah actually has God singing over Israel—a magnificent revelation![4] Listen to the Psalmist as he sings:

> When I consider your Heavens,
> the work of Your fingers,
> the moon and the stars
> which you have set in place...[5]

At the moment the Psalmist must have been looking up at the night sky, just as you and I have often done. He was enraptured by the sight of God's majestic workmanship. Is it possible that the music of the spheres somehow entered his soul? In a later psalm he sings,

> The Heavens declare the glory of God; the
> skies proclaim the work of His hands.
> Day after day they pour forth speech; night
> after night they display knowledge.[6]

Now the Psalmist seems to be responding joyously to what he is hearing. Again, was it perhaps the music of the Heavenlies? It is a fact that some of the most beautiful music ever composed is based upon the Psalms.

Now for the surprise.

The theory of a divine melodious harmony of the spheres may not appear in current scientific textbooks, but it has intrigued the imaginations of thinkers, poets and wise men down the centuries. Pythagoras, a Greek mathematician and one of the greatest of the ancient teachers outside of Palestine, set forth the idea brilliantly five and a half centuries before Christ. What we know about him is what his followers have left to us, since he reportedly never wrote anything.[7]

Pythagoras seems to have been a fascinating character and, in his day, a superb scientist. His mathematical discoveries surpassed anything in the ancient world. He said that the Earth was spherical, not flat; that it not only rotated on its own axis, it orbited with the other planets as part of the solar system. He also forbade his disciples to eat beans and had some off-the-wall ideas about reincarnation.

Pythagoras established a colony of followers in southern Italy where he made his remarkable scientific deductions. He contended that the Earth was somehow affiliated with the sun, the moon, the other planets and stars—in fact, the entire cosmos—in an immense divine harmony. As the celestial bodies moved through their orbits, he said, they emitted music. This is the first known reference to "music of the spheres" in recorded history.

Two centuries later Aristotle rejected Pythagoras' idea, but Plato warmly embraced it in his *Republic,* and so did the Roman orator Cicero in his century, as he wrote in "The Dream of Scipio." Hippolytus, an early Christian leader in Rome, a scholar and martyr (c. 236 A.D.) wrote this about Pythagoras and his theory:

"Pythagoras...having made a profound study of the nature of number(s), asserted that the cosmos sings and is harmoniously constructed, and he was the first to reduce the motion of the seven planets to rhythm and melody."[8]

In the climax to his description of Paradise in the *Divine Comedy,* the poet Dante (1265-1321) declared that he heard the whole of creation singing praises "to Father and to Son and Holy Ghost" as the "great wheels" of the universe turned. He wrote that the sweet music overpowered his senses with "inebriate rapture."

Two centuries after Dante, Shakespeare elaborated on the Pythagorean theory of celestial music in his drama, *The Merchant of Venice.* In the play's final act he created a sentimental moonlight scene in which Lorenzo speaks these words to his beloved:

> Sit, Jessica. Look how the floor of heaven
> Is thick inlaid with patines of bright gold;

> There's not the smallest orb which thou
> behold'st
> But in his motion like an angel sings,
> Still quiring to the young-ey'd cherubims:
> Such harmony is in immortal souls;
> But whilst this muddy vesture of decay
> Doth grossly close it in, we cannot hear it.[9]

What Shakespeare was saying is that the stars and planets do in fact sing "like angels," but our mortal ears are so "muddy" we can't hear their harmony. Pythagoras himself, centuries before, had given a different kind of response to the question: *If the stars give off music, why can't we hear it?*

Pythagoras explained that we humans couldn't hear the melodies of the Heavens because they have been sounding in our ears from birth and we don't notice them. In the same way, he said, a coppersmith fails to notice the banging noises around him all day while he is working at his trade.

Cicero drew a different illustration from his knowledge of life in Egypt. He wrote that people who live within sound of the cataracts of the Nile river are unconscious of the noise the waterfalls make in their ears. I shall add a third illustration: Americans who leave their television sets turned on all day are very apt to be oblivious to sounds coming from the set!

Sir Thomas Browne in his *Religio Medici* (1643) claimed that there was "soundless music" in the spheres,[10] and Percy Shelley, the Romantic poet, wrote just before he died (1822) about "sweet planetary music."[11]

What does all this tell us about the character of the Creator? I can only speak for myself: It tells me that at the time God created the heavens and the Earth, He was motivated by joy. That joy caused the universe to come into being. That is why the stars sang and the sons of God shouted in their elation.

So the universe is not a random assortment of atoms and fiery globes spinning and whirling in empty space to their destruction. Rather it is a symphony of rhythm and harmony that expresses the pleasure of its Creator in the way He shaped it. In other words, divine joy was and is the primal reason for its existence. And, one might add, for ours also.

I have read the opening chapters of Genesis to learn whether the sacred record shows that some other motive was involved in the work of creation. Again and again I have asked myself, "Why was the Lord God doing this? What was in His mind?" Reading the mind of the Maker is something for which I have neither skill nor aptitude. Yet the text as I understand it clearly implies that God Almighty was enjoying Himself as He fashioned the Heavens and the Earth. Everything He made He saw was "good" and the total result He declared to be "very good."[12] The way God blessed the birds, the animals and fish; the tender interest and solicitude He showed in creating a mate for our first parent, give us unmistakable clues to the love and joy behind the divine design.

This is the God and Father of our Lord Jesus Christ, who sent His Son into the world to establish a Kingdom of love and joy. The Bible tells us that "God so loved the world that He gave us His only Son, that whoever believes on Him should not perish but have everlasting life."[13] That life Jesus Himself described in explicit terms: "I have come that they might have life, and have it abundantly." Another translator uses the expression "to the full."[14] There is no way life can be lived to the full apart from joy.

Do the Heavenly bodies send out music? It beats me. But a time would eventually come when the Great Musician would pour His music into my soul, and fill me with joy in the knowledge of His salvation. That same joyful knowledge set Paul and Silas to singing hymns after they had been stripped and beaten, and while they sat in stocks at midnight in the dungeon of a Philippian jail.[15]

Let this chapter on music and joy close with some lines by the poet Henry van Dyke, based on the "Hymn to Joy" in the choral movement of Beethoven's Ninth Symphony:

> Joyful, joyful, we adore thee
> God of glory, Lord of love;
> Hearts unfold like flow'rs before thee,
> Op'ning to the sun above...
> All thy works with joy surround thee,
> Earth and heav'n reflect thy rays,
> Stars and angels sing around thee,
> Center of unbroken praise."[16]

---

[1]Job 38:7.

[2]*International Standard Bible Encyclopedia,* Grand Rapids, Eerdmans, 1988, Vol. IV, p. 611. Cf. also Isaiah 40:26.

[3]Franz Delitzsch, in Keil & Delitzsch, *Commentary on the Old Testament,* Grand Rapids, Eerdmans, Vol. 4, 1986, p. 315.

[4]Zephaniah 3:17.

[5]Psalm 8:3.

[6]Psalm 19:1.

[7]Cf. W.K.C. Guthrie, *History of Greek Philosophy,* Vol. 1, "The Earlier Presocratics and the Pythagoreans," Cambridge University Press, 1967.

[8]Guthrie, op.cit.

[9]*The Merchant of Venice,* Act V, Scene 1.

[10]Sir Thomas Browne, *Religio Medici,* in Harvard Classics, New York, P.F. Collier & Son, 1909, Vol. 3, 9, p. 338.

[11]Percy Shelley, "Epipsychidion," in *The Poetical Works of Shelley,* Cambridge ed., Boston, Houghton Mifflin, 1975, p. 300.

[12] Genesis 1:31.

[13]John 3:16.

[14]John 10:10.

[15]Acts 16:23.

[16]From *Poems of Henry Van Dyke,* New York, Scribners, 1911.

ANOINTING

Armin Gesswein, one of the great prayer warriors of the twentieth century, recently called my attention to an expression in the first chapter of the Letter to the Hebrews. The eighth and ninth verses read:

> But to the Son He says... "You have loved righteousness and hated lawlessness; therefore God, your God, has anointed you with the oil of joy more than your companions."

Of course I had read the verses before. I just had never let them become part of me. As I checked out the passage, word after word, the text seemed to be saying that God's Son, Jesus Christ, had a more joyous spirit, a merrier disposition, a heartier laugh, and a more lively sense of humor than any of His disciples. When the truth sank in I felt like throwing my hat in the air, the problem being that I wasn't wearing a hat.

Stop and think of what those words could mean to us in our Christian witness today! Try this tack. For a moment let's forget about responsibility, obligation, requirement, duty, and all those guilty ought-to-be-doing words that we often associate with religion. Instead, let's pick up on that awesome question the apostle Paul threw out in his letter to the Christians of Galatia: *"What has happened to all your joy?"* And then note his other question in the same letter: "After beginning with the Spirit, are you now trying to attain your goal by human effort?"[1]

Life whizzes by so fast. We spend our waking hours struggling to "make ends meet," eating, rushing here and there, making up for what we should have done yesterday. Then here comes a Man who looks upbeat and cheerful, and he says to us, "Let's go. Follow me. I've got some good news. We'll have a ball!" And He is neither an ogre nor a threat nor a new kind of legalistic cult leader with some wacko rules. He's just the Savior of the world, the Redeemer of the lost, and He wants to anoint us with the oil of joy.

Why oil?

It's a good question. When the author of Hebrews wrote those great words, "God, your God, has anointed you with the oil of joy" (or, as the older translation reads, "the oil of gladness") he was saying simply that the Father had equipped His Son Jesus with (among other things) a jubilant personality.

So why are oil and joy linked together? Because oil in the Bible is the visible sign of an invisible inner joy, as in the act of anointing. Thus the Psalmist sings:

> How good and pleasant it is
> when brothers live together in unity!
> It is like precious oil poured on the head, running down on the beard...[2]

In many ways oil and joy have an identical effect on human life. They actually do the same things, the only difference being that one operates in the material environment, the other in the spiritual.

Let's see how this works out. We shall begin by looking at what role oil filled in ancient Palestine, where it was used as a commodity.

In Bible times oil—usually olive oil—was extremely popular. King Solomon carried on a flourishing trade in olive oil with Tyre and Egypt. Olive oil was used extensively for just about everything: for ceremonial rites, for cooking, for lamp fuel, for internal and external medication, and cosmetically for anointing the head and body after bathing. Giant olive trees from the time of Christ are still producing fruit in Jerusalem's Garden of Gethsemane. A huge olive press from the past may be seen today at the site of what was once Bethany.

Several hundred years before Christ, the prophet Isaiah linked oil with joy in a classic passage, declaring that the Spirit of God had sent him to comfort all who mourn in Zion, and "to bestow on them the oil of joy instead of mourning." The same usage, if not the same words, is found in the Psalms, most notably in Psalm 23:

> You anoint my head with oil;
> my cup overflows.
> Surely goodness and mercy will follow me
> all the days of my life...[3]

Oil and joy just seem to go together.

Now let's look at life in the Nineties. Oil has become the most important commodity in the world. It makes everything happen. It was the hidden stake in the Persian Gulf war. Can you imagine life in America today without oil? If the Earth were to cease yielding up its oil—and the resource is not infinite—the human race would virtually shut down. Perhaps we should exempt Holland, where everybody rides bicycles, and remote parts of China where the wheelbarrow is still the prime mover. And of course we should never forget our friend the horse.

But let's think about joy. It does the same things oil does, but on quite a different plane. It lifts the human spirit, thereby greatly improving health. It lightens the burden of work, making the daily load easier to bear. It improves relationships between people, and thus makes life worth living.

Oil makes things run smoothly. When it is poured on a waffle iron, it keeps the batter from sticking to the plate. When poured into the groove of a sliding door that sticks, it makes the door open easily. When poured into the crankcase of a car, or the oil pit of a giant turbine, it makes the machinery operate.

Joy does the same thing. A kitchen hug makes the breakfast waffle taste better. A cheerful spirit makes the trip in a car, a ship or an airplane pleasant. Oil provides the base for perfumes which in turn provide delightful aromas. Joy brings a fragrance to life all its own which no perfume can match. You think with horror of what the world would be like if there were no oil to run it. Can you imagine what the world would be like if all the joy were taken out of it? We would work and work, and scrimp and scrimp, and earn and earn—for what? To buy food to eat and clothes to wear and beds on which to rest, so we could go back to work. God help us.

Another property of oil is that it reduces strain.

As a young newspaper reporter I became the proud owner of the sweetest little automobile these hands have ever driven. It was a 1935 Model A Ford roadster, yellow with red wheels and a rumble seat. Today, restored, it would no doubt claim a fortune. I bought the car in Seattle in 1938 and drove it to California, where I hoped to write a book. One weekend I drove into the Sierra Nevada foothills to a village named Tuolumne. Object: to track down an old girlfriend who was teaching school there. Result: mixed.

While returning to the Bay Area on Sunday afternoon my little car broke down somewhere between Sonora and Oakdale. I checked the gas tank; it was nearly full. A kind passing driver with a rope towed me into Oakdale where a fat garage man gave me the news: My car was ruined. A connecting rod had rammed through the block. Trying to save a few pennies on a downhill run, I had neglected to fill the crankcase.

No oil! My feisty yellow roadster came to grief because without oil there was no protection against the strain of the engine's functioning. Cylinders, pistons, valves, rings, all quit. In the same way oil leaks in giant airliners can lead to disaster and tragedy because of metal strain.

Today we live in a world where oil spills are creating a lot of trouble, but spills from a tanker cause nowhere near the kind of strain that would result if there were no oil at all. We know that the Earth holds only so much oil. My mishap on the Big Oak Flat Road could have been prophetic of the future.

Joy works the same way. A joy-filled Christian can take knocks and setbacks better than a skeptic or a crape-hanger. Remember the famous Murphy's Law? "If anything can go wrong, it will." Well, suppose it does! It takes a better and more positive attitude than that to climb back after life has slapped us down. A touch from God can do for morale what complaining and the "cynic's ban" can never do.

Time and again we find in the Psalms that when things became desperate, the Psalmist reached for the joy of the Lord.

> I said, this is my infirmity: but I will remember the years of the right hand of the Most High.[4]

In his distress of mind he reached for the goodness of the Lord, and the joy came back.

In his second Letter to the Corinthians, the apostle Paul shows us vividly the effect of joy on trouble. Paul describes a vision he had fourteen years earlier in which he was "caught up to the third heaven." It was a time of rapture, of inexpressible ecstasy and "surpassingly great revelations." But this awesome experience was followed by extreme bodily pain, a "thorn in the flesh" that would not go away. Paul was forced to cry out to God for deliverance. God's answer was, "My grace is sufficient for you; my strength is made perfect in weakness."[5] Because the oil of joy was still being poured out on God's servant, he could survive the pain and come up smiling.

So here is what the Bible teaches: Joy does for the human soul exactly what oil does for the human body and its environment. Joy makes hard tasks easy. It turns duty into pleasure. Let's say your front lawn, like mine, leaves something to be desired and requires work. The thought of such labor makes you think about going shopping or playing a round of golf. But on reflection you realize how blessed you are to have a home with a lawn; you see how gracious God is to give you health; furthermore, the exercise turns out to be exactly what you need. So you lay it on; and if determination makes the work a piece of cake, joy adds the icing. That evening you have a tremendous appetite for dinner.

Joy not only turns duty into pleasure, it changes tears into smiles. Blaise Pascal, the French scientist, made a written record of his own spiritual encounter with God, and sewed it into the lining of his coat, where it was discovered after his death. In it were the words

Joy, joy, joy, tears of joy[6]

and that's what happens. After we let go of our lives, God takes hold and the tears we are shedding become tears of joy.

Jesus Christ Himself had something important to say about oil and joy. He told a story about ten bridesmaids. This story has puzzled scholars and translators for many years. I shall presume to tell it to you my way. The ten girls were waiting for the bridegroom to appear, according to a kind of game or custom that still exists in Palestine.[7] They had been with the bride as it was the night of the wedding feast, a very special and joyous event. Each bridesmaid had a lighted lamp, for according to the game plan they were to wait outside the house. There they would meet the bridegroom when he arrived and escort him inside where his bride and the guests were waiting. But the bridegroom was long in coming (as usually happened) and the bridesmaids fell asleep. Then midnight came, and the cry went up that the bridegroom had arrived.

The bridesmaids awoke. Five of them found their lamps had used up their oil. The other five girls had brought extra fuel in vessels but there was not enough oil to go around. To be out at night with no lighted lamp was against the law.

As a result, only five bridesmaids met the groom and escorted him into the house. The rest missed him because they were out after curfew looking for oil. When they finally came back they tried to get in the house but were denied entrance. Too late. No oil, no admittance, no wedding, no joy.

Inside, a celebration, laughter, singing, music, dancing, feasting. Outside, cold.

Such is life. We live on a planet running out of resources and rocketing through the cold and darkness in outer space; but inside the Kingdom of God there are resources abundant, together with light, joy and merriment.

How's your oil?

---

[1]Galatians 4:15, 3:3.

[2]Psalm 133:1-2.

[3]Psalm 23:5-6.

[4]Psalm 77:10.

[5]2 Corinthians 12:2-9.

[6]Emile Cailliet, *The Clue to Pascal,* Philadelphia, Westminster Pres, 1943, pp. 67-68.

[7]Matthew 25:1-13. Cf. William Barclay, "The Gospel of Matthew," *The Daily Study Bible,* Edinburgh, St. Andrew Press, Vol. 2, 1963, pp. 352-53.

FEELING

Harry Lauder, the Scottish comedian, wrote a song, "I Love a Lassie," in which a timid middle-aged man relates his frustrated effort to marry a younger woman. He says he had "known her ever since she was a baby"; but when he screwed up his courage and proposed to her, she gave him a withering look and replied, "Marry yew? A thing like yew? Never!"

It sounds cruel, but the truth is a lot of non-Christians feel that way about Christians who try to evangelize them.

A retired elder in Leavenworth, Kansas, once told me, "The prayer meeting is the beauty parlor of the church." Here is a likely seat of trouble, for a large percentage of churches no longer hold prayer meetings. A bright spirit, a merry heart (such as Jesus had), a vital, living faith, and a contagious enthusiasm have always been among the prime requisites for winning people to Christ. The radiant joy of the Holy Spirit shining in the face of a believer will pierce the religious fog in a friend's mind better than any number of sermons from the pulpit.

Without that joy, the Gospel of Jesus Christ will never break down the resistance of our skeptical generation. All the ardor, the fervor, the devotion and the prayers of the faithful may well fail to penetrate today's unbeliever *unless the Gospel message carries the same note of joy it had when it was first proclaimed.* Fear won't do it. Wrath won't do it. Arguing won't do it. Pleading won't do it. Joy will do it. Because Satan is on a rampage and the Christian faith is under deadly assault, many earnest evangelicals are telling us that we must fight back. We must "defend the Bible." But Charles Spurgeon retorts, "Defend the Bible? I would as soon defend a lion." Righteous anger is not the strongest weapon in God's armory. Joy is.

What do any of the life goals we set for ourselves amount to if they do not bring personal satisfaction and joy? What does salvation itself, the very heart of the Gospel message, mean to us if all the enjoyment it promises is taken away? If there is no joy in Heaven, who wants to go to Heaven? We can thank God for the word of inspiration He gave to David:

> In Your presence is fullness of joy;
> At Your right hand are pleasures forevermore.[1]

A young woman wrote me, "There's a special type of joy I have experienced that reaches the point of elation when someone to whom I have witnessed accepts the Lord as Savior. The most elated moment I can recall was when my husband accepted the Lord as his Savior. That day I rejoiced with the angels of God."

A young man wrote, "Whenever I am thanking God for saving me, I experience joy that feels like a well of water springing up inside me. It is the only pure feeling I've ever had."

A middle-aged woman wrote: "Yesterday my heavenly Father said to me, 'What would be your pick if I were to let you have what you wanted most of all?' I looked over all His good things and said, 'Lord, it all looks good, but I want You to choose for me what You think I need most.' He smiled and said, 'I think that most of all you need some joy. Open your mouth wide and I'll fill it.' And didn't I open it wide, and didn't He fill it though! He just poured and poured until it was running over and outside. All the empty places of my life just soaked up joy and more joy. I took the whole bottleful." That woman had been ill for eighteen months.[2]

Does the joy of one's salvation make the believer feel any different? The answer of Scripture is Yes. Body therapy is part of the ministry of the Holy Spirit. "Fear the Lord and shun evil," says the Proverb. "This will bring health to your body and nourishment to your bones."[3] The jubilation, the glorious sense of freedom that comes supernaturally with the assurance of our redemption in Christ is no bubbling "Schweppervescence." When we fully grasp its significance, salvation does a lot more than make our feet want to dance.

The Name of Jesus means "God saves." Saves from what? From sin to a life of righteousness and from grief to peace and joy. But God doesn't stop there. He wants to pour out His Holy Spirit into every fiber of our being, infusing a glow that penetrates to the bloodstream, the joints and sinews and muscles and tissues. He wants to affect the emotions and rejuvenate the mind, so that our brain cells react to the joyous message. Whatever our bodily condition at the moment, just thinking about Jesus has its beneficial consequences. God wants us to revel and exult in what has taken place in our lives, and He expects the assurance of our salvation to produce joy in others.

One of the most important things joy does is to put a smile in our witness. It enhances the play instinct, produces a lot of fun, and makes us laugh. A sure proof that Jesus laughed is the fact that those whom He has saved laugh a lot. Why not? When you are filled with joy it's hard to keep from smiling or laughing.

Sixteen hundred years ago the venerable John Chrysostom confessed that in spite of his efforts to maintain holy solemnity in worship, his great cathedral in Antioch often rocked with laughter, "even during the very time of prayer." The "golden-mouthed" one told his congregation he saw no harm in laughter as such, for he insisted that "laughter has been implanted in our soul, that the soul may sometimes be refreshed." He just didn't appreciate people laughing "beyond measure and out of season," particularly when he was in the pulpit praying for them.[4]

What makes us laugh? Children do. Jesus seems to have spent a lot of time with children, for He knew their games and quoted them. Animals make us laugh. The ridiculous situations in which we sometimes find ourselves make us laugh. A really hilarious story will make us double up with laughter.

Perhaps what makes believers laugh the longest is to think of the predicaments we used to be in, the quandaries and dilemmas and jams and blue funks, so many of them caused by our own stiff-necked pride or stubborn bullheadedness. We laugh because the hurts that sting so, the slights and buffets from other people, no longer devastate us the way they once did, praise God. They still come; we are still vulnerable; but we can laugh because God has delivered us from such nonsense, has sealed us with His Spirit and made life a joy to live in His Presence. We laugh because Jesus has broken the chains of death and has assured us of the delectable richness of the joys of Heaven. We are home free, accepted into the Kingdom of Love and adopted into God's royal family. Roll the drums, sound the horns and ring the bells, the party has already started!

> I'm living on the mountain, underneath a
> cloudless sky;
> I'm drinking at the fountain that never shall
> run dry,
> I'm feasting on the manna from a bountiful
> supply...[5]

The joy of salvation not only makes a Christian laugh, it makes him or her sing. For many centuries during the Dark and Middle Ages, the lovely music of the church did not always reflect the joy of the Gospel. Whatever the reason was, the present musical situation in the church today is in better and healthier balance.

Gospel songs began to appear in the nineteenth century and gave worshipers a chance to express their enthusiasm and delight in the assurance of their salvation.

> If you want joy, real joy, wonderful joy—
> Let Jesus come into your heart![6]

Music lovers have sometimes expressed distress at the rhythmic tunes and popular melodies of the gospel song, but the truth is that the joy of redemption in Christ cannot be contained. It keeps breaking out in warm, lively music. When the Jesus Movement of the late 1960s and 1970s emerged on the West Coast of America, it developed its own style of worship. Some of it was lively, but much was based on the Psalms as they appear in the traditional King James version.

A beautiful collection of praise choruses has resulted, giving full expression to the joy of salvation in Christ:

> I love you, Lord, and I lift my voice
> to worship you, O my soul, rejoice!
> Take joy, my King, in what you hear:
> May it be a sweet, sweet sound in your ear.[7]

This is not a book about miracles, but joy has a way of bringing to pass physical changes that defy explanation apart from taking the supernatural into account. Norman Cousins has ably demonstrated on a secular level the therapeutic powers of laughter.[8] The relationship of the joy of salvation to improved physical health is a field that needs to be explored in depth. One thing is certain: Jesus Christ still heals, and whether the healing comes to the Christian through medication, or divine intervention in natural processes, or through the saving balm of joy, it is all from His gracious hand.

People who have the joy of the Lord in their hearts tend to look different. Any doctor, any psychologist, any employer will validate the fact that a joyful, lighthearted spirit produces an attractive personality. Why belabor the point? A radiant face, young or old, beautiful or not, invites a pleasant response. "The light of the eyes rejoices the heart."[9] The brightness of the eyes lights up the face, and the goodwill of those who see it, Christian or not, is strengthened. The contours of the face remain the same, but the smile adds a touch of glory.

The actual, original wording of Psalms 42:11 and 43:5 reads, "I will yet praise Him, the salvation of my face and my God." Dr. Martin Lloyd-Jones says the psalmist is telling us, "When I really look at God, as I get better, my face gets better also."[10]

God gave us our faces, took great pains with them, and wants them healthy. He wants them to be smiling reflections of His own joy, so that others will not only hear our Christian testimony but will actually see it when they encounter us face-to-face. Something indefinable but beautiful then passes between us, and ordinary-looking people suddenly become very attractive. It's true!

When joy comes into our lives we not only feel better and look better, we act better. Franz Josef Haydn composed some of the most beautiful sacred music the world has ever heard. He once wrote, "When I think of God, my heart is so full of joy that the notes leap and dance as they leave my pen."[11]

The best way to find that joy is to get into a place where the Lord God can use us. The patriarch Abraham once commissioned his old servant to find a wife for his son Isaac. This bride was not to be local, but was to be brought from Haran. It meant the servant had to mount a camel and ride across Mesopotamia to Haran. He made the journey and fulfilled his commission by bringing back Rebekah. He explained his success this way: "I being in the way, the Lord led me."[12]

Jesus was filled with joy in the Holy Spirit as He went through Palestine from place to place, feeding the hungry, relieving the poor, offering hope, healing the afflicted, reuniting families, forgiving sin, raising the dead, and always refusing to make distinctions based upon race, color or language. The apostle Paul spelled out the fruit of the Spirit in his letter to the Galatians: "Love, joy, peace, patience, kindness, goodness, faithfulness, gentleness and self-control."

If you read between the lines of the New Testament, if your senses are fully alive as your eyes follow the text, you may make a wonderful discovery. It is that the atmosphere around Jesus and the disciples in Palestine was charged not only with the redemptive message of faith, hope and love, but also with laughter, music and joy. That's right! Tambourines, flutes, trumpets, lyres, harps, cymbals, zithers and bells—all were there in Galilee, and you had better believe they followed after Jesus as He made His electrifying tour in the early days of His ministry.

The purpose of a vine is to produce fruit. John Wesley said the purpose of a Christian is to do all the good we can, by all the means we can, in all the ways we can, in all the places we can, at all the times we can, to all the people we can, as long as ever we can.[13] And I would like to add, do it for Jesus, do it with joy, and if you can, have some fun doing it.

In a real sense we can't keep joy; it must keep us. Joy is an elusive thing, a vapor, a poem, a hummingbird. Because it is a slice of eternity, it won't fit into a self-storage warehouse; but when we give it away it comes back to us—in buckets of delight.

Paste this scale of values on your refrigerator door:

Love is better than hate.
Joy is better than grief.
Faith is better than doubt.
Courage is better than fear.
Truth is better than falsehood.
Righteousness is better than sin.
Peace is better than war.
Hope is better than despair.
Kindness is better than cruelty.

Freedom is better than slavery.
Right is better than wrong.
Good is better than evil.
God is better than godlessness.

Then choose the better.

---

[1]Psalm 16:11. The apostle Peter quoted this passage in his address at Pentecost. Cf. Acts 2:28.

[2]Testimony of Phyllis Grey, published in the *Log of the Good Ship Grace,* Haven of Rest Ministry, Hollywood CA, Vol. 19, No. 12, April, 1953. Used by permission.

[3]Proverbs 3:8.

[4]Homily 15 on Hebrews in "Works of John Chrysostom." *Nicene and Post-Nicene Fathers,* 1st Series, edited by Philip Schaff, New York, Christian Literature Co., Vol. 14, 1890, p. 442.

[5]From the hymn, "Dwelling in Beulah Land," by C. Austin Miles, 1911.

[6]From the chorus, "If You Want Joy, Real Joy," by Joseph Carlson.

[7]Chorus by Laurie Klein, © 1978, House of Mercy Music (Administered by Maranatha ! Music c/o The Copyright Co., Nashville, TN.) All rights reserved. International Copyright secured. Used by permission.

[8]Norman Cousins, *Anatomy of an Illness,* New York, W.W. Norton, 1979.

[9]Proverbs 15:30.

[10]D. Martin Lloyd-Jones, *Spiritual Depression: Its Causes and Cure,* Grand Rapids, Eerdmans, 1965, p. 12.

[11] *Topical Encyclopedia of Living Quotations,* eds. Wirt and Beckstrom, Minneapolis, Bethany House, 1982, No. 1810.

[12]Genesis 24:27.

[13] *Topical Enyclopedia,* op.cit., No. 3480.

TAKING

Jesus had just completed a sensational preaching tour of Galilee, and word of His ministry was now spreading over Palestine and Syria with the speed of a Santa Ana brush fire.

"He has come!"

"Who?"

"The man."

"What man?"

"The man of God."

"The Messiah?"

"We don't know, but hurry. We want to see."

"Why? What is He doing?"

"Healing everybody. Come!"

And they came. He returned to the area of Capernaum to find the crowds larger than ever. Amid the shouts and excitement Jesus spoke to His disciples, and they followed Him up the mountainside. There on a spot overlooking the beautiful lake, He seated Himself and began to teach them.

Let's open our New Testament to Matthew 5 and examine the first word Jesus spoke: "Blessed." It is a noble English word, and it has been used for centuries. But is it really interesting to people today? I sense that in the Nineties the English word *blessed* seems to have lost a bit of its sheen. Like the other English word *rejoice,* most churchgoers don't use it much outside of church. When they do, it has a way of branding a person as "religious," and many Christians don't like that.

What does it really mean? It means "favor from God." Thus the Old Testament records that Isaac called down favor from God on his son Jacob.[1] In the New Testament, Jesus stood on the Mount of Olives and called down favor from God on His disciples.[2]

Now let's look at the way *blessed* is used in the ten verses that follow, which are known as the Beatitudes. Here Jesus is using the word as a descriptive adjective, as a way of emphasizing the *rewards* he was setting forth. The Beatitudes as a whole are really portrayals of positive human attitudes and lifestyles. Jesus is proposing behavior that He promises will ultimately produce love, joy, peace, and all the marks of the Kingdom of God.

So what does the word signify here? It seems to imply a slightly different level of meaning from "favor with God," one that relates directly to the point Jesus is making. Many translators have recognized this, and are obviously dissatisfied with *blessed* as a translation. Some have substituted the word *happy,* which is a far cry from Isaac blessing Jacob. Thus we find "Blessed are the poor in spirit" becoming "Happy are the poor in spirit."

Clearly such expressions will not do what they are supposed to do in today's linguistics. To be poor in spirit is not exactly to be happy. What's happening? Let's try another Beatitude: "Happy are they who mourn." That proves to be even more inept, for it is a contradiction in set terms. Whoever heard of a happy mourner? *Happy* is most certainly an awkward substitute for *blessed.*

Thus the word *blessed* in the context of the Beatitudes is too religious for some, while the word *happy* is too secular for others. What to do? What English word can we find that would more nearly clarify and convey Jesus' meaning?

In this connection Gerhard Kittel's *Theological Dictionary of the New Testament*[3] contains an interesting statement by Professor Friedrich Hauck of Erlangen, Germany. I quote from Dr. Geoffrey Bromiley's translation: "The special feature of the term *makarios* [blessed] in the New Testament is that it refers overwhelmingly to the *distinctive joy* which accrues to man from his share in the salvation of the Kingdom of God." *That's it!* What Jesus was describing in the Beatitudes was neither an Old Testament blessing nor the fleeting contemporary notion of happiness, but rather a deep "distinctive joy" which He promised to those who participated in the "salvation of the Kingdom of God." Let's experiment with the idea. Here is how the Beatitudes would sound with such wording:

"Let the poor in spirit *take joy,* for theirs is the Kingdom of Heaven."

"Let those who mourn *take joy,* for they shall be comforted."

"Let the meek *take joy,* for they shall inherit the earth."

"Let those who hunger and thirst for righteousness *take joy,* for they shall be filled" (with that joy).

"Let those who are merciful *take joy,* for they shall obtain mercy.

"Let those who are pure in heart *take joy,* for they shall see God."

"Let those who are peacemakers *take joy,* for they shall be called sons of God."

"Let those who are persecuted for righteousness' sake *take joy,* for theirs is the Kingdom of Heaven." Note how this rendering matches the two verses that follow:

"*Take joy* when they revile you and persecute you and say all kinds of evil against you falsely for my sake. *Be joyful and exult,* for great is your reward in Heaven, for so they persecuted the prophets who were before you."

Yes, exult. Shout. Leap. Dance. Laugh. Away with all this long-faced sobriety that Jesus shunned! Away with false reverence and manufactured intensity in dealing with sacred matters. As C. S. Lewis remarked to me in our 1963 interview, "There is too much solemnity about, too much speaking in holy tones."[4]

How then does this fresh rendering of the Beatitudes relate to people who are under enormous pressure, who are facing troubles that seem insurmountable? How do they relate to the Christian wife whose husband has just announced that he is leaving her? To the teenage youth who has just been dropped from the squad after being elected captain?

I suggest we examine the text.

"Let the poor in spirit take joy, for theirs is the Kingdom of Heaven." "Poor in spirit" can mean many things, including a sense of failure, self-pity, hopelessness, depression, a lack of faith and self-confidence. But Jesus is saying precisely, *"Not to worry."* He is saying that poverty of spirit is God's way to joy. As the late Dr. Harold Ockenga once explained, "In order to be filled with the Spirit we must meet God's conditions. To begin with, we confess to God that we are *not* filled with the Spirit."[5]

To be emptied of human spirit is exactly what is needed before a person can receive a fresh filling of the Holy Spirit. So take joy. Take courage and hope. The Kingdom of Heaven lies before you.

"Let those who mourn take joy, for they shall be comforted." Of course we should mourn when we have suffered a loss. If we don't—look out! Mourning is God's provision, the natural response to the tragedies of life. If a sorrowing father tries to put on a brave front after burying his beloved daughter, he only complicates the functioning of the delicate bodily system. Tears are God's healing balm in times of grief. Eventually the mourning season will end and the pain subsides. God will send comfort and restoration. The joy will come back. When it comes, take it.

"Let the meek take joy, for they shall inherit the earth." Meekness is seriously misunderstood in today's society because people are always confusing it with timidity. Bunkum! When a soldier salutes his superior, is that being timid? Consider the illustration of a shut door. Three persons wish to go through it: one is aggressive, one is timid, and one is meek. The aggressive person, sure that it is locked, kicks the door down. The timid person isn't sure whether it is locked and stands in front of it, afraid to test it. The meek person tests the door to see whether it is unlocked. If it is, he opens it and walks through. That is why the meek shall inherit the earth.

"Let those who hunger and thirst for righteousness' sake take joy, for they shall be filled." This Beatitude can be reduced to one word: "Excelsior!" Or in the more modern idiom, "Go for it!" A Christian young man I knew expressed it well: "I have changed my address, folks. I used to live on Broadway, but I've moved over to Straight Street. If you want to do business with me, you'll have to come to where I live." To get on track for God, we have to realize there is a right way and a wrong way. Choose the right, hunger for it, thirst for it. The promise is that we will be filled with the Spirit and with joy.

"Let those who are merciful take joy, for they shall obtain

mercy." Jesus does not mean, "Do this and you'll get that." To make a bargain with God one must have something to bargain with, and if we had anything to bargain with we would not need His mercy. Our repentance is no asset, for it is the liquidation of all our assets. God's mercy belongs to Himself, and He exercises Crown rights over what is His own. What Jesus is really saying is that God wants merciful people, so He can fill them with joy.

"Let the pure in heart take joy, for they shall see God." Purity of heart is not the commonest characteristic of the human species. Just as we think we have them licked, our old temptations keep coming back. Ah, what hypocrites we are! What shall we do? For us followers of Christ there is only one recourse:

> I must needs go home by the way of the
> Cross, there's no other way but this.[6]

If we confess our sins He is faithful and just to forgive us our sins, and to cleanse us from all unrighteousness.[7] So take joy! From joy comes purity of heart. Jesus knew: He was also tempted.

"Let those who are peacemakers take joy, for they shall be called sons of God." Once in Scotland I stopped two wee lads who were fighting furiously in an Edinburgh street. I did it by giving them each a penny. (They were big coppers.) When I suggested that the boys shake hands, they fell into each other's arms and then went off laughing to spend their lucre. Unfortunately when it comes to adults and nations, bribes won't make a cease-fire; the rancor is too deep. God is the only real Peacemaker. He sent His Son Jesus Christ to make peace through the blood of the Cross.

That is our message. History proves to us that martial victories fail to bring either peace or joy to the world. Jesus Christ brings both.

"Let those who are persecuted for righteousness' sake take joy, for theirs is the Kingdom of Heaven."

Madame Jeanne Marie Guyon wrote, "When once we have enjoyed God and the sweetness of His love, we shall find it impossible to relish anything but Himself."[8] What makes that sentiment unusual is that Madame Guyon spent thirty years in confinement for her faith, including eight years in the notorious Bastille in Paris. To undergo persecution and still be able to take the joy of the Lord—that is what this Beatitude calls for.

John Frith was a godly young Englishman who became a martyr in 1533. Frith had helped William Tyndale translate the Bible, and had denounced unbiblical teaching respecting the Lord's Supper. For that He was condemned to death by none other than the British lord chancellor, Sir Thomas More. In his classic *Book of Martyrs* John Foxe stated that John Frith took his stalwart and joyful faith with him to the bonfires of Smithfield, outside London.[9] He was just thirty years old.

As the second Fruit of the Spirit after love, joy thus becomes the true reward in each Beatitude. Jesus offers this joy to us as a gift of love from God the Father. The Psalmist expressed it well:

> Delight yourself in the Lord
> and He will give you the desires of your heart.[10]

Then joy will become the ensign flying over the battlements of your heart to signal that the King is in residence.

---

[1]Genesis 28:1.

[2]Luke 24:50.

[3]G. Kittel and G. Friedrich, eds., *Theological Dictionary of the New Testament,* tr. by Geoffrey W. Bromiley, Grand Rapids, Eerdmans, Vol. IV, 1967, p. 367.

[4]Cf. C. S. Lewis, *God in the Dock, Essays on Theology and Ethics,* Walter Hooper, ed.), Grand Rapids, Eerdmans, 1970, p. 259.

[5]Harold J. Ockenga, "The Third He," in *Decision* magazine, January, 1969, p. 15. © 1969 by the Billy Graham Evangelistic Association.

[6]From *The Way of the Cross Leads Home,* words by Jessie Brown Pounds, 1906. © 1972 by Alfred B. Smith.

[7]1 John 1:9.

[8]Mme. Jeanne Marie Guyon, "Short and Very Easy Method of Prayer," in *Spiritual Disciplines,* S. E. Wirt, ed., Westchester, IL, © Crossway Books, 1983, p. 172.

[9]John Foxe, *Acts & Monuments of the Church, Containing the History & Sufferings of the Martyrs,* London, A. Fullerton & Co., 1850, Book 8, pp. 524-29.

[10]Psalm 37:4.

YOU'VE GOT IT!

Neil Armstrong was out in space a quarter of a million miles, taking his spindly *Eagle* down to a landing on the moon, when he found his vehicle approaching an uneven, rocky piece of the satellite. It was a critical situation that called for quick action. He steered the craft to a more level surface, using up most of his allotted fuel but touching down safely.

When you arrived on the shore of Joy Country, you may have selected a difficult site. You found mountains too rugged to scale and side trails blocked by slides. All passages to the higher meadows of delight were cut off. Now, studying your chart, it appears you should have established your staging area on Love Beach. Why? Because the joy that God offers is always contingent upon His love. In other words, joy in God is inaccessible by itself. One can have love without joy, but one cannot have joy without love.

You don't know how much fuel you have or how much time is left. The meadows of joy are there, the excursion boat is docked, the celebration is ready and waiting.

Let's pause a moment for prayer. Let's draw together our thoughts, go over what we have learned, and see if we can establish a few succinct, overarching principles that will help take us where we want to go.

1. *God created joy because He is Himself joy.* The universe itself is an extension of that joy. Regardless of the evil we meet every day, regardless of suffering and disease, the fact remains: we exist because God took pleasure in creating us. Wrath and judgment came later in the creation process, as the Bible makes clear. Love and joy were there first.

2. *Our supreme vocation in life, our* raison d'être, *is to reflect the joy of the Creator.* This is done by the Holy Spirit Himself working in and through our lives. The Holy Spirit is love seeking to spread joy, and He works only in minds and hearts that are uncontaminated by other spirits.

3. Jesus Christ *came to us bringing the Glad Tidings of salvation.* He taught, He healed, He loved, He spread joy, and so began the greatest movement the world has ever seen. He went to the cross of Calvary to take away our sin, rose from the grave, and lives now in the everlasting joy of Heaven. But before He left, He told us His joy would remain with us, and that someday He would come for us.

4. *There is nothing wrong with Spaceship Earth,* apart from what has been transpiring on its surface. In its revolving and orbiting through the solar system our globe is right on time, meeting its schedules with exact and flawless timing just as God ordained it, along with the rest of the celestial bodies in the universe. This is the *divine harmony of creation* that gives birth to music, a special gift of joy to us from the same Creator who gives us life. We know from Scripture that some day there will be a new Heaven and new earth.

But until then
my heart will go on singing.[1]

During a long period in my own Christian life my tank was empty, but I didn't know what to do about it. I tried earnestly to maintain a respectable profile, reading my Bible daily, praying, teaching a Sunday School class, staying away from temptation. As a Christian I knew I was supposed to radiate joy, but gave up on it. At the time it seemed impossible; certain people had treated me too badly in the past. The hurt was too deep. So I allowed resentment and bitterness to fester within my heart. From my perspective there was no point in telling those who had mistreated me that I had forgiven them. They would have promptly replied that they had done nothing that needed forgiveness. Obviously my opinion differed.

In spite of my eagerness to serve Jesus, there were people I simply could not love unless they changed. Never once did it occur to me that *I* needed changing. My sympathies were with the man who told A. B. Simpson, "I don't want to love some people. I should not respect myself if I did. I take a real pleasure in disliking them."

The result was that in the depth of my heart, where I should have reveled in the joy of God's salvation, a vacuum existed. The true essence of the Christian life had escaped me. The cause of my misery was private, but the fact of it was devastating and inescapable. It had spoiled my outlook to the extent that I had actually lost interest in living. Scientists say that nature abhors a vacuum, and the same is true of the spiritual life.

About this time (1971) a friend, Leonard Ravenhill, wrote me that a revival had broken out in a Canadian city. My journalistic duties took me there, and I arrived with a tape recorder. The story of that revival has been told elsewhere at length;[2] my purpose is simply to relate some things that occurred one night in Winnipeg, Manitoba.

The minister, Wilbert McLeod, declared that the Holy Spirit is love. I had thought myself fairly well acquainted with the Holy Spirit, but this was new. I had heard the Holy Spirit called power, fire, unction, wisdom and a mighty rushing wind, among other attributes; but not love. The preacher made it clear: God is love and the Holy Spirit is God. I completed the syllogism.

Mr. McLeod went on to say that to be filled with the Spirit is to be filled with love. This also was new. He was talking not about the gifts of the Spirit, but rather about the filling and the fruit. He said if I wished to be filled with the Spirit I would have to deal with my problem. (How did he know I had a problem?) The way to deal with it was to give it to God, who would take it—and me—to the cross. There I could ask God to crucify me.

Mr. McLeod explained that crucifixion with Christ means the end of all effort and striving; it means brokenness before the Lord at Calvary, dying to the sinful attitudes that have taken root in our lives, and the utter emptying of self. He said when he himself had reached that end, he experienced a filling of the Holy Spirit without even asking for it. Four weeks later the Canadian revival broke in his church.

Many times I had read the apostle Paul's statement that he was crucified with Christ[3] but never fully understood what he meant. Now I was learning that a person cannot understand the cross unless he or she has been there; but after I had in fact gone there myself and felt the nails, I could ask God to fill me with His Spirit and He would do it. I could even thank Him in advance for doing it.

Mr. McLeod said one other thing that stuck in my memory. He said, "You can't change anybody, but God can change you."

A few weeks later during a prayer meeting at which some friends from Canada were present, I asked for prayer and was taken to the cross. There I was at Calvary, identified with Jesus, stripped as He was stripped. It was more than a metaphor; clearly I had nothing. My resumé was blank, my soul was empty. Jesus, I knew, had died for my sin. Now I gave up on my self, for it had abysmally failed to produce what the Bible commanded. This was no religious experience; rather it was the bottoming out, the nadir of all such experience.

Several days later I was surprised to discover that the bitterness and rancor in my heart had disappeared. The Lord Jesus Christ had quietly sent the love of God into my heart by the Holy Spirit, and all the hurt that had accumulated over many months and years had evaporated. Even my marriage was turned around.

I couldn't believe it, but it was true. I had nothing against anybody. I recalled hearing a Canadian lady say, "God sent a divine solvent into my heart and dissolved the bitterness I had built up against my husband over twenty years." Strangely, I was also reminded of the Cheshire cat in *Alice in Wonderland*.[4] It sat on the limb of a tree and smiled until gradually it vanished and only the smile remained. I too felt things were vanishing until I was left with nothing but a smile; I now loved everybody.

It took three years before I understood from the Word of God what had happened to me. And what does it all mean to you, who may or may not have been brushed by revival, but are just as keen as I was to get to the mountain meadows of Christian joy? It means that joy, like everything else in the Christian life, begins at the cross. Until the sin question has been dealt with, all we are doing is playing tic-tac-toe with life. But the old gospel hymn said it well: "There is room at the cross for you." Once we are broken and emptied, we can be filled—and not until.

We are now living in the Nineties, but western Canada still enjoys the blessings of the revival. Teams of Spirit-filled Christians continue to crisscross North America with a message of spiritual awakening and love, and thousands of believers have come into new joy in the Lord. Count me one.

So our search for joy in this life and beyond ends where it begins, with Jesus. Moving inland from Love Beach, we follow an easy trail to the mountain meadows and lakes. The peak of sin is a peak no more. It has blown its cap, thanks to the blood of the Lamb. The crag of stress is diminished by Him who assured us that His yoke is easy and His burden is light. The massive rock face of adversity disappears in the distance through the Word of Him who spoke of moving mountains. It is still true that weeping remains for a night, but joy comes in the morning. Finally, the sharp peak of pain no longer obstructs the path to joy, for the heart is healed by the touch of the Lord Jesus whether or not the pain lingers.

But how do we keep the joy, once it comes? We don't; it must keep us. C. S. Lewis reminds us that joy is a "desire turned not to itself but to its object."[5] We find joy in our children, our grandchildren, our brothers and sisters, our nieces and nephews, our parents, our grandparents, our friends, and all those who look upon us in love.

We find joy in our pets, our native land, the glory of hills and sky, the warmth of the sun, the freshness of the wind, the trees, the singing of birds, the fruit of the fields—but most of all, we find our joy in Jesus, the Master of wind and wave, the Lamb of God slain for us, and our Savior.

In one of T. S. Eliot's best-known poems, the rather priggish lover J. Alfred Prufrock declaims, "I have measured out my life with coffee spoons."[6] Coffee spoons? Beloved, when the Holy Spirit pours the love of God into your heart, don't be surprised if huge containers of joy come rolling down the driveway of your soul and into your life.

As you make your way toward the high ground of Joy Country, don't look at the crags or anything else—look at Jesus. But hold on! The topography seems to be changing. Turn around. It's not the configuration of the land, but the topography of your face. I see something there I didn't see before. Praise the Lord. Go take a look in the mirror.

By George, you've got it!

---

[1]From the song, *Until Then,* by Stuart Hamblen.

[2]Cf. Erwin Lutzer, *Flames of Freedom,* Chicago, Moody Press, 1976.

[3]Galatians 2:20.

[4]Lewis Carroll, *Alice's Adventures in Wonderland,* Garden City, N.Y., Nelson Doubleday Publishers, n.d., p. 67.

[5]C. S. Lewis, *Surprised by Joy,* New York, Harcourt, Brace Publishers, 1956, p. 220.

[6]T. S. Eliot, *The Love Song of J. Alfred Prufrock.*

PART TWO

Some Marvelous People of Joy

Billy Graham and Grady Wilson
Corrie ten Boom
Pecos Higgins
Francis of Assisi
Brother Lawrence of the Resurrection
Billy Bray

Billy Graham and Grady Wilson

Evangelist Billy Graham once remarked to me that at any given time four books were being written about him. Now several of those books repose on a shelf in my library. Recently I researched them for information about two aspects of Billy's personality: his inner joy and his sense of humor. One delightful insight is revealed in John Pollock's first biography of Dr. Graham, published in 1966. It quotes a 1937 letter written to his mother from Tampa, Florida, where Billy had just enrolled in a Bible College. He wrote:

> Mother, words can't express Florida Bible Institute . . . I never felt so close to God in my life . . . This is the first time I have enjoyed studying the Word of God . . . I love it here. I am stronger and feel so much better.[1]

It is disappointing to me that not much else has appeared in his biographies about either Billy Graham's personal joy or his sense of humor. The indexes do not mention either subject, and the pages of the books say little. In an earlier book[2] I mentioned that the bursting joy that characterized Jesus of Nazareth in the early days of His ministry seems to be underplayed by His chroniclers and translators. Now I find that the portrait of Billy Graham found in current books and periodicals misses the vibrant, captivating spirit of the man himself. And since no one else at the present time of writing seems to have expressed an opinion publicly on this subject, I shall be bold to speak out.

Billy Graham is probably the most gracious person I have ever met. In the forty years since I was introduced to him at a ministers' meeting in Oakland, California, in the fall of 1954, he has done things for me that leave me everlastingly grateful. He is the one person in the world who, after the Lord Jesus Christ and my own intimate family, has been my truest and most wonderful friend.

In December, 1958, Billy Graham telephoned me at our home in East Oakland, California, where I was pastoring a lively church and enjoying it. He said he was planning to launch a new Christian magazine and wanted to know if I would consider becoming the editor. It happened I had just finished writing a book about his San Francisco crusade earlier that year. What followed can be told in one sentence. Our family moved to Minneapolis, headquarters of Billy's ministry, and during the next seventeen years *Decision* magazine grew to become the largest Christian monthly periodical in the world.

When I listen to Billy preach as I still do, and hear the tributes that are paid to him by princes of the church and world leaders, I remember the fun times our team had traveling from continent to continent with the simple message of the Gospel. I think of the sheer joy I felt at being with a company of thoroughbreds engaged in the greatest work on earth: the winning of human souls into the Kingdom of God.

My work as editor brought me into close contact with Billy on occasion. I remember times when we prayed together in Australia, ate together in Florida, worshiped together in San Francisco, rode together in Tasmania, visited together in South Africa and Brazil and other places. I remember when my wife and I were guests in his home at the invitation of his charming wife Ruth.

Ruth Bell Graham is a nonpareil in her own right. She is an equally inspiring person, a highly successful wife and mother, a brilliant author and speaker—and a lot of fun. She beautifully complements her husband's ministry and has her own winsome approach to life. In Taiwan I have visited a Christian college girls' dormitory built by her and bearing her name; but to describe her works is to resort to Biblical words like *sixtyfold* and *hundredfold.*

As for Billy, the good cheer he radiated then and still radiates is part of the invisible cord that binds together not only his family but his team and staff and friends. We would do anything for him.

It is common to hear friends who have known Billy well remark that his platform presence and his natural walk are indistinguishable; that on or off stage he is the same person. I consider the statement correct but incomplete. It fails to tell us what that "same person" is really like. Billy Graham, even though he preaches a message dealing with life, death and eternal destiny, or perhaps because of it, is basically a lighthearted individual, genial and fun-loving. The cares of this world, the ever-increasing woes of humanity, the burdens of being a herald of the Almighty, while taken very seriously, rest lightly on his shoulders. It is a gift of sheer grace, for Billy knows far more about ill-health and human suffering than do most people. He has seen it around the world and has experienced it in himself and in his family.

To apprehend this aspect of Billy's personality—so different from many of the world's leaders—one needs to study not only Billy himself, but the message he preaches. Jesus said, "My yoke is easy and my burden is light,"[3] and Billy takes our Lord at His word. In his first book, "Peace With God," one of the more important books of the mid-century, he wrote,

> One of the characteristics of the Christian is inward joy. No matter what the circumstances, there will be a joyful heart and a radiant face. So many Christians go around with droopy faces that give no outshining glory to God. Upon meeting a Christian it is easy to tell whether or not he is a victorious, spiritual, yielded Christian. A true Christian should be relaxed and radiant, capable of illuminating and not depressing his surroundings. The Bible says, "For the joy of the Lord is your strength."

In the same book Billy spoke of Heaven as being "a place of joy, service, laughter, singing, and praise to God."[4] In a sermon published in *Decision* magazine in 1967 he wrote,

> In all ages people have found it possible to maintain the spirit of joy in the hour of trial. In circumstances that would have felled most men, they have so completely risen above them that they have actually used the circumstances to serve and glorify Christ. I have found in my travels that those who keep Heaven in view remain serene and cheerful in

> the darkest day. In these times of upheaval and uncertainty, the trustful and forward-looking Christian remains optimistic and joyful, knowing that "if we endure, we shall also reign with Him."[5] (2 Timothy 2:12.)

People who earn their living traveling are fully aware of human deficiencies, foibles, and shortcomings. Itinerant evangelists are no different; and yet Billy Graham seems always charming, smiling, enjoying life, happy to meet new friends and to go out of the way to pray with or offer help to someone. Billy is as quick to laugh as he is to pray. He is not above teasing gently as he is not above expressing love and appreciation. Even when he is part of a group dealing with a problem, he leaves the people involved in an upbeat mood that reflects the man himself.

I have read three extremely critical books about Billy Graham. The authors (two American, one British) have accused him of a number of things I know to be untrue. That is not to say that the man is without fault; who is? I am quite satisfied that Billy Graham is as fallible as the rest of us. I am equally sure that his weaknesses, such as they are, are not worth writing books about.

When the final biography of Billy Graham is written, I hope it includes more than how great he was as a person, how unsullied his integrity and how wide his influence upon his generation. I hope it goes beyond his devotional life, his daily reading of Psalms and Proverbs, his generosity, his visits to the White House, and his affection for his family and for those serving with him in his worldwide ministry. I hope it also talks about his genial personality and his refusal to take himself seriously. I hope it mentions the press conference in Copenhagen when Billy was asked by a rather ungracious newsman, "What's so special about you?" and he replied, "There's nothing special about me." I hope it describes his smile, his laugh, his easy, uncomplaining, light spirit as he goes through life touching and helping people of every age and color.

In younger days Billy preached like an Old Testament prophet, and his words were surgically sharp as he inveighed against sin. Yet even then in his personal relations he was the soul of pleasantness and kindness. Today he is more mellow and speaks more slowly, but the message of redemption from sin and reconciliation to God through Jesus Christ is crystal clear as ever.

In 1987 in Charlotte, North Carolina, a man passed away who shared Billy Graham's ministry intimately for several decades. He was Dr. Grady B. Wilson, a boyhood friend who later became Billy's first associate evangelist and a lifelong comrade in the work of the Gospel. Grady's departure from this life was mourned by thousands all over the world.[6]

In addition to his other admirable qualities, Grady, with whom I was privileged to have a close friendship, had a superbly developed sense of humor with a Southern flavor, a gift that made him friends on six continents. The fact that he traveled side by side with Billy everywhere says much about Grady's qualities. It also says something about Billy's own temperament. Billy liked having Grady around. He brightened everything. Grady also had a keen instinct for crowds. He could assess the way a meeting was going, and was invaluable in spotting irregularities from the crusade platform.

It might be said that every evangelist ought to have a Grady Wilson on his team to keep him and everyone else cheerful and chuckling, but that would be impossible; Grady was without peers. Let me share with you a brief note I received from Grady dated May 18, 1962, a year and a half after I began editing *Decision* magazine. Better than I can say, it reveals the kind of men I worked with:

> *Dear Woody:*
>
> *Everywhere I go people are commenting on your masterful presentation. Coming back from Florida, Billy remarked that you were God's man for the job. Keep it up and more power to you! We love you much and thank God that He sent you our way.*
>
> *Your devoted friend,*
> *Grady*

That letter is pasted in my Bible. To me it is more than a model of encouragement. It tells me indeed that I am doing acceptable work but it also tells me that I am loved.

To know Grady Wilson, his wife Wilma and their daughters, was to feel in the depth of one's heart the genuine charm of the Christianity that expressed itself on the Billy Graham team.[7] I came as an unknown from the West Coast to join a group that had been world famous for ten years, and was made welcome.

What was Grady's humor like? In 1954, when Billy's historic London Crusade was in full swing in Harringay arena, a country vicar demanded to speak with Billy. Grady expressed regrets and suggested "another time." The man then adopted a hostile stance.

"What are you Yanks doing here anyway?" he asked.

"We're here because a thousand clergyman invited us,"

Grady responded.

"Well, I wasn't one of them. You came over on the *Queen Mary,* a big, expensive ship. I suppose you came first class. Have you Yanks never read that our Lord Jesus Christ came into Jerusalem lowly, riding upon an ass?"

"Yes," Grady replied, a twinkle in his eye, "and if you find me an ass that can swim the Atlantic, we'll be glad to make use of him."

Grady Wilson not only lightened the whole atmosphere of the evangelistic enterprise, he represented a side of Billy Graham's own character that gets little attention. Grady was no court jester; his role was far more significant. He drew out the delightful side of Billy: the merry side.

Billy Graham did not hesitate to use a good story in his preaching when it was appropriate, sometimes to help an audience to relax, sometimes to illustrate a point, and sometimes to counter the adulatory expressions that often swirled about him. He liked to tell about his riding in an elevator with two other men, one of whom was his friend. The other gentleman remarked that he heard Billy Graham was in the building, and Billy's friend told him that the man was actually standing next to him. The gentleman turned, sized up Billy and remarked, "My, what an anticlimax!"

The very existence of humor in the thousands of sermons now in the archives of the Billy Graham Center at Wheaton, Illinois, makes it evident that Billy Graham differed from some great soul-winners, not to speak of the theologians of the past. Humor was not a noticeable part of the repertory of John Calvin, John Knox, John Wesley, Charles Finney or Reuben Torrey. Humor was, however, used effectively by Martin Luther, Ulrich Zwingli, Hugh Latimer, John Bunyan, George Whitefield, Dwight L. Moody, Sam P.

Jones, Charles Spurgeon and Billy Sunday. Billy Graham belongs with the latter group and so does Grady Wilson. Both men had many characteristics in common with the great Christian leaders of the past; a lively sense of humor is only one of them.

One final word about the man William Franklin Graham. He is aware that Christianity is no longer popular, if it ever was, among certain elite groups in America. He also knows that Christians endured horrible persecutions in the past, and may well face them in the future. But the joy in Billy's heart is built on a foundation different from popular acclaim. It rests on the promises of God revealed in His Son Jesus Christ—promises of forgiveness, personal guidance and eternal bliss to all who believe in Him.

---

[1]John Pollock, *Billy Graham, the Authorized Biography,* London, Hodder & Stoughton, 1966, p. 30.

[2]S. E. Wirt, *Jesus, Man of Joy,* Nashville, Thomas Nelson, 1992.

[3]Matthew 11:30.

[4]Billy Graham, *Peace With God,* New York, Doubleday, 1953, p. 81.

[5]"Joy in Tribulation," *Decision* magazine, June 1967, p. 1. © 1967 by the Billy Graham Evangelistic Association. Used by permission.

[6]Cf. Grady Wilson, *Count It All Joy,* Nashville, Broadman Press, 1984.

Corrie ten Boom

"I cashed the check of Romans 5:5: 'The love of God is poured out into our hearts by the Holy Spirit which is given to us.' "

As Corrie ten Boom spoke those words to the 1974 International Congress on World Evangelization in Lausanne, Switzerland, she captured the imagination of 4,000 Christian workers drawn from 151 countries around the world. She also unknowingly drew aside a veil that had shrouded the most baffling mystery of my life.

I had met Corrie a few times during her active years prior to her death in 1983 on her 91st birthday. As editor of *Decision* magazine I had published her work. Recently I have enjoyed reading a number of her books as well as those written about her.[1] One significant fact kept coming to light: again and again she referred to the above words of the apostle Paul, which I had heard her quote in Lausanne about the outpouring of God's love into our hearts by the Holy Spirit.

For Corrie it was an inspired word that enabled her to counsel many bitter souls, and more specifically to shake hands with two of her tormenters at the Ravensbruck Nazi concentration camp for women, both of whom had come to meetings after the war to hear her speak. One had been a prison guard and the other a Gestapo nurse. They asked her to forgive them for the way they treated her and the other prisoners, one of whom, Corrie's sister Betsie, died at their hands.

Instead of simply complying with their requests, Corrie "cashed the check" of Romans 5:5 and in each case the Holy Spirit gave her a fresh outpouring of love and joy. As she traveled to over sixty countries around the world during the next three decades, she apparently used the verse over and over in counseling inquirers and in speaking to different groups. She made a special effort to visit prisons, and talked with many who found it impossible to forgive those who had wronged or hurt them. She told of one woman, an ex-prisoner who came to one of her meetings and later prayed, "Thank You, Jesus, for Romans 5:5 that brought into my heart God's love through the Holy Spirit. Thank you, Father, that Your love is victorious over my hatred."

In her notebook Corrie wrote, "How I love Romans 5:5. I use it often."[2]

Today the memory of Corrie is enshrined in the hearts of thousands of people around the world who loved her. She was not just an energetic older woman with a passion to talk to strangers about Jesus. She was human, could be cranky, had her bad moments, but she was a fun person. She liked to tease and to engage in banter. She had a hearty Dutch laugh. Her travels occasionally landed her in difficulties, but many times she found amusement in the midst of her predicaments.

Corrie never forgot what she and her sister went through in the prisons of Holland and Germany, but she learned to season those memories in the joy of the Lord. Let me quote from Corrie's description of a prison she visited in Rwanda, Africa, which demonstrates how she used her victory over the experiences of Scheveningen and Ravensbruck to minister to those in many lands still in confinement.[3] She writes:

It was almost the worst prison I have ever seen. It was a small building, but many prisoners were sitting outside on the ground.

"Where do you sleep at night?" I asked.

"Half of us sleep inside, the rest must stay outside because there are too many prisoners."

It was all so sad. The ground was one large pool of mud, for there had been a tropical rainstorm. Some men had branches on which they sat, others had banana leaves or pieces of newspaper. Their faces showed anger. How could I bring them the Gospel?

On this day I said, "Lord, give me a message for these men that will help them."

Then the Lord said, "Speak about joy."

"Lord, how can I speak about joy to these people who live in this terrible place?"

The answer was, "My Holy Spirit is here in this place, and the fruit of the Spirit is available wherever you are."

I said, "Lord, give me an ocean of joy to share with these poor fellows." And I remembered that when I had been in prison I had found joy even in the midst of the most desperate surroundings. When we are powerless to do anything, it is a great joy that we can step inside the ability of Jesus.

Then I heard myself giving a very happy message in that prison. The faces of the men lit up when I told them that the joy of the Lord can be our strength, even when we are in very difficult circumstances.

I told them, "The only thing necessary to begin moving into the joy of the Lord is to tell Jesus Christ that you would like to be His follower. Receive Jesus Christ as your Savior and Lord, and He will give you the joy." When I spoke of Jesus who is good and strong and so full of love, who never leaves you alone, and who has an answer for all the problems of sin and death, I could almost shout for joy.

Many did respond to Jesus. I could see it in their faces; but I also saw faces of people who were not ready or willing. They remained just as dark and unhappy as before.

I said to them, "Fellows, I can understand that you think such joy is not possible for you when you are in this prison. You may be saying, 'This is not for us, our lives are too terrible.' But I can tell you that I was in a prison where it was worse than here, and where ninety-five thousand women died or were killed, including my own sister. There I experienced that the Lord Jesus is always with me. His Holy Spirit lives in my heart. He has never left me alone.

"There is joy for you, too, but you must be at peace with God and man—that is possible! When you confess your sins to the Lord, He is faithful and just, and He forgives you. He removes your sins. He cleanses your heart, and He fills you with the Holy Spirit. The fruit of the Spirit is joy."

By this time it was pouring rain, but I realized that the joy of the Holy Spirit can be experienced in all circumstances. "Who will open the door of his heart to this Friend and Savior, Jesus?" I asked. All of them, including the guards, put up their hands, and their faces were beaming.

I saw that this time it was real for all of them. When I went to the car to leave, all the men and guards accompanied me to the street. They were shouting something which I could not understand. I asked the missionary who was my interpreter, "What are these men saying?"

She laughed and said, "They are all shouting, 'Come

again, old woman. Come again and tell us more about Jesus.' "

Then the missionary told me, "I have stopped my visits here, it seemed so hopeless. Now I have seen what the Holy Spirit can do, I will come back every week."[4]

—

That is just one story that Corrie ten Boom told as she traveled through six continents, smiling, laughing, exhorting, relating anecdote after anecdote. Always she would look for those who had been shut away from society, and would tell them that she, too, had been shut away. Then she would add that the Holy Spirit who brought the joy of Jesus to her and Betsie at Ravensbruck would do the same for them in their confinement.

It is not for me to tell of the way God used Corrie's ministry in the latter years. The books she wrote, the films she made, the counseling she provided from her home in Placentia, California, the magazine she published, the staff she assembled, the Christian honors that came to her, are for others to record. Her biographer, Carole Carlson, relates an incident that occurred when the water heater in her home burst and firemen were called. As Corrie stood watching the firemen work their pumps, she said to them, "Do you men know Jesus Christ? He is a friend of mine, and I'd like to introduce Him to you." Carole adds, "The firemen kept on working, no doubt thinking, 'What kind of nut is this old lady?' " But for Corrie it was simply following the call of God she received when her sister Betsie went from Ravensbruck to be with the Lord.

In her little volume, *Clippings from My Notebook,* Corrie reflects on the meaning of joy.[5] She writes:

Sometimes the responsibility of all my work has burdened me. There is so much to do, and we all understand that we must redeem the time, because the days are evil. What joy that we may and must surrender everything.

When I talked over my concern with the Lord, He showed me an empty suitcase. He said, "You possess nothing, you have surrendered all, so you have no responsibilities at all. I carry all responsibilities, you are only my steward."

What joy came into my heart! I prayed, "O Lord, let me see You a moment."

"Look at your left hand," He said.

I saw that my hand was in another hand. That hand was pierced . . . it was Jesus' hand. I never understood before what surrender meant—our weak hand in Jesus' strong hand! His strength in our life! Surrender to the Lord Jesus is dynamic and relaxed. What joy! Hallelujah!

—

Please excuse my taking the liberty of intruding myself, the author, at the end of this profile of Corrie ten Boom. I do it, as Archibald the All-Right did in the Gilbert & Sullivan operetta *Patience,* "on compulsion." Miss ten Boom's use of Romans 5:5 gave me a Scriptural insight into a puzzling change in my own life that had taken place two years earlier. In Chapter 10 I described my attendance in 1971 at a revival meeting in Winnipeg, Manitoba.[6] At that time I could not understand what had happened to me or how it could have happened.

In 1974, as I looked into my little Greek-English New Testament, in Lausanne, Switzerland, I found the words *poured out* in Romans 5:5. Poured out! A cascading of love from Heaven. I thought, as the Lord lives, that's what happened to me two years ago! Now I understand why all my bitterness just evaporated in thin air. The Holy Spirit poured out the love of God into my heart and brought me joy instead of malice and resentment.

The mystery was clarified. What God did for Corrie ten Boom, He did for me. I felt like standing on my chair and announcing to the entire Lausanne International Congress on World Evangelization, "Corrie is telling the truth! It works! What happened to her, happened to me!"

No wonder Corrie took that verse with her around the world and used it so often. No wonder she became known as a woman of joy! Perhaps some may object that she put too great a strain on a single verse of Scripture. That is because they don't realize she was dealing not with mere sentences, or with ink and paper, but with the Word of God which is living and active and sharper than any double-edged sword. J. B. Phillips once said that when he was translating the New Testament he felt like an electrician who was under a house repairing wires when he suddenly got hold of the mains!

When I first told fellow Christians about the peace and joy that came into my heart and drove out all the animosity that had clogged my spirit for so long, some of them assured me it was "just yielding" on my part. I knew they were wrong; I had tried that route and found it blocked by my own unwillingness. Now for the first time Corrie showed me the truth from Scripture; it was an actual invasion of the Holy Spirit, pouring out God's love, peace and good cheer into my joyless heart. And He is still pouring it out! That is the real secret of the Christian life.

---

[1]For a bibliography of writings by and about Corrie ten Boom, apply to Pamela Moore, curator, Corrie ten Boom Collection, Dallas Baptist University, 3000 Mountain Creek Parkway, Dallas TX 75211-9299.

[2]Corrie ten Boom, *Clippings from My Notebook,* Thorndike, ME, Thorndike Press, 1982, p. 126; also see pages 23, 82, 115.

[3]Corrie ten Boom wrote the story of this visit in at least two of her books. To provide fuller detail, I have sought to combine the stories without altering her words.

[4]Carole Carlson, *Corrie ten Boom, Her Life, Her Faith, a Biography,* Old Tappan, NJ, Fleming Revell, 1983, 210. Used by permission.

[5]Corrie ten Boom, *Clippings from My Notebook,* op.cit., pp. 155-56.

[6]See page 79.

Pecos Higgins

We are going out on the drive, cowboys,
you know that starts the battle—
This time we are rounding up Souls of Men
instead of the longhorned cattle.

—Pecos Higgins

No one ever knew his real name. He was born on the Gulf Coast of Texas in 1883, and moved with his parents to Breckenridge and then to Pecos. At six years of age some of his associates got him "dog drunk." While still small, he began to work on ranches up and down the Pecos river, punching cattle in the mesquite thickets. He had eight months of actual schooling, but he became the most colorful Christian cowboy poet in the history of the West.

In his early twenties Pecos Higgins (as he liked to call himself) moved into Arizona and lived out his days there and in New Mexico, not counting jail time and two terms spent in the Texas state penitentiary at Florence. In 1907 he was invited by the Miller Brothers to join their "101 Ranch Wild West Show" on a tour of North America and Europe.

During his overseas travel Pecos, who was now a skilled rider, performed along with Tom Mix, the cowboy actor, before Kaiser Wilhelm II of Germany in Berlin. He also had an unusual encounter with His Royal Highness Edward VII, King of England, Scotland and Wales, Sovereign of the British Empire, Emperor of India, Defender of the Faith, etc. He told the story often:[1]

> The king was at a reception of some kind in London, and I went in there because I wanted to see him. I walked up to him and said, "Are you the king?" Everybody else seemed scared of him, but I wasn't. He put that thing in his eye [a monocle] and said, "My word! Are you a Yankee?" I said, "I am." "Well," he said, "I'm the king."
>
> I told him that I had one of the best pitching horses in the world, and that we were in a show called "Bugjumpers." I invited him to come down to see me ride that horse. He did, and my pony acted just as rank as he could get. I put on the best show for that king he ever did see, and afterward I talked to him over a drink and he said, "Oh, that horse is a good bugjumper, he's a good bugjumper."

The drink that Pecos had with the king of England was a portent of disaster. His friend Joe Evans says in the years that followed Pecos "drank enough whiskey to fill Elephant Butte Dam." He married and divorced five times, sold liquor to Indians, put together his own six-shooter before anyone in Texas had seen one, cussed and gambled and shot his way through half a century. He ended at last at age 71, a battered, hopeless, drunken wreck whom Christian friends found lying on a cot in an abandoned ranch in

Arizona. They said he looked as if "every bone in his body had been broken," and "he walked like an old stove-up cow pony."

How this man became as well-known as any cowboy in the real west (that is, east of Hollywood) and a popular speaker at campfire meetings in half a dozen states, can only be explained in the dimensions of a higher Power. An explosion of joy filled his heart and never left it for the next 17 years, from 1955 until his homegoing in Prescott, Arizona in 1971 at 88 years of age. The story of his turning to Jesus Christ is best told by Pecos himself in letters he wrote to his Christian cowboy friend Joe Evans, who had known him for several years. The first letter was written from Wild Cat Camp, Arizona, in February, 1956:

Dear Friend Joe:

I want you to know that I started crawling through the fence last August to get on the other side, when the nice people came and hunted me up and took me to a little camp meeting over west of here at Burton. They told me it was your wish that I should go, and I am so thankful that I did so, but more thankful to you that you took all the pains in the world in my behalf.

I got through the fence last Sunday on the safe side, and joined the church at Alpine near Springerville. Rev. Otis Spriggs sent you a wire about it that night. [The telegram read PECOS HIGGINS SAVED.] Gene Pugh was preaching at the time, and will be here for me at five o'clock this afternoon to take me in to be baptized tomorrow, Sunday.

Joe, I hope no living person ever runs the narrow risk I did, not finding out something about the Lord. I can look back and see where He helped me a million times when I was working against Him. And I did not know enough then to thank Him and give Him credit for it.

Cowboy, I enjoy them letters of yours and you don't know how much you have done for me. You are the starter of this NEW LIFE of mine—and I mean NEW. This is the happiest week I have ever spent. My work has gone better and everything is fine and I have something to look forward to in the end. It is the only week I have ever spent letting the Lord be my pal. Thanks a million to you and all God's other nice people. With love and many blessings, your friend, Pecos Higgins.

In another letter he wrote:

Dear Friend Joe:

Since I joined up with the Lord and you fellows, boy, I am living the new life just as good as I can make myself know how. I study it just like I did bronc riding and how to outfigger them old outlaw cattle in the rough mountains and deep canyons.

I am trying the same system on a bunch of my old friends in these parts. I have never had the pleasure of carrying a soul to the Lord yet, though I am a new hand. I must try to get at least one notch on my gun this year.

Now, Joe, I am going all the way with the Lord and you church folks. I am going to make a hand. I went all the way when I was working for the Devil. Outside of hi-way robbery and murder, the Devil can't say I ever backed up at anything there was to do. I started on the bad side from a small boy and of course I was with the lead of the drive all the time. I knew all the ropes and shortcuts and it was easy for me to stay there.

But I have got tapped off a long ways behind on the good side of the fence. Now I am whipping and spurring and riding a good horse and with God's help and all you good people's help I will catch up.

I feel now like I imagine a little hound pup does when his eyes first come open. I can see things and kinder want to bark. I am longing for that camp meeting in July more than I ever wished for those times when we would all go into town for the big roping contests and see the wild boys and girls. I would go back to the ranch half dead, broke, in debt, and really did not know what all had happened. I will leave the next camp meeting with a lot different feeling to that, Joe.[2]

—

Later, in a talk at a laymen's conference in Wheaton, Illinois, Pecos elaborated on the subject:

There were a lot of people at that camp meeting [at Burton, Arizona] and an awful lot of prayer. After supper they fixed me a seat right up by the Amen corner, and Gene Pugh preached. About two or three weeks later I came to the Lord, joined the church and was baptized.

I wanted to do it. There wasn't anybody to persuade me to do it. I worked and studied her out myself. Whenever I make up my mind to do something I always do it. I've been happier all the time ever since. Always glad I done it. But of course the Lord is the one that done it.

It happened almost overnight, and for the last several years everything has gone good for me. I just turned over my life altogether. Now I live a different life. I'm as happy as a fed pig in the sunshine. I never get into any trouble or anything. I can see the good in everything and everybody.

I used to couldn't see the good in nothing much. I haven't found a person I didn't like, since then. It used to be I disliked all but a few. I never thought about nobody else either. But I have been a different person ever since, gone with different people. I couldn't run with people that I run with now, and do like I was doing.

We sure know that the Lord exists, and the Bible says He is right with you from the time you want Him. He'll sure do it. You won't have to do it. I don't see how people can keep from living a Christian life now. Of course I don't tell them that, because at one time you couldn't talk to me about it. I wouldn't stay where you was at. But that was because I didn't have that feeling. Today I can't understand why a person wouldn't give his life to Christ.[3]

—

Joe Evans described Pecos as "one of the wildest mavericks we've ever roped and branded." He told a story about meeting Pecos shortly after his conversion when he came to visit Joe and got off the train at Big Spring, Texas. It seems Pecos had a habit for years of carrying a pint bottle of whiskey in his boot, and he even carried it to the church in Burton when he was taken there for the first time by his friends. On this occasion as Pecos stepped off the train in Big Spring, Joe Evans noticed with dismay a bulge in Pecos' boot and asked him about it. Pecos reached down and pulled out a copy of *The Baptist Standard,* a Texas publication. Joe commented, "That seems to tell the story better than I can write it.[4]

Pecos' joyful spirit and picturesque cowboy language soon made him a popular figure on the Christian camp meeting circuit. Joe Evans took him through eighteen cities in the eastern United States, and everywhere the church people adored him. In the summertime the two old men toured the "Cowboy Camp Meetings" in Wyoming, Colorado, Texas, Oklahoma and other states, and each evening they would stand at the campfire, swap stories and "do their act." Invariably Pecos stole the show, as he was a natural entertainer and could recite poems by the hour.

In 1959 Pecos was taken to Wheaton, Illinois, and introduced to the crowd at a Billy Graham evangelistic crusade on the Wheaton College campus. I met Pecos there for the first time, and when in 1962 Billy Graham came to El Paso, Texas, I learned that Pecos was then living in Prescott, Arizona. A friendly Christian airplane pilot offered to fly to Prescott and bring Pecos to the Crusade meeting. I had the pleasure of welcoming Pecos and Joe Evans one day on Billy's platform. Later *Decision* magazine carried Pecos' story, and for several years thereafter the two veteran cowboys continued their visits to the summer cowboy camp meetings, witnessing to their Lord before the folks gathered in the evenings around the campfire.

In earlier years Pecos had sometimes dabbled in ribald verses, writing with a pencil on whatever paper he could find. Now as a Christian he had been handed the greatest theme of all, and he grasped it with delight. Eventually Joe Evans collected a sheaf of Pecos' quaint verses and published them as *Pecos' Poems.*[5] All of his verses centered on the Lord Jesus Christ, and one poem in particular was a favorite with his audiences.

Years later, in 1992, I had the privilege of visiting the Pioneers Home of Arizona in Prescott, where Pecos resided from 1962 until his death in 1971. A few of the current residents remembered him. They spoke of the smile they said he always wore, even when suffering acutely from arthritis.

If ever I knew a man who enjoyed knowing and loving God, it was this wild, cantankerous outlaw. But I only knew him after Jesus had tamed him and made him into a godly cowboy poet and a delightful human being. Here is the poem which he titled, "Looking for Work."[6]

Dear Lord up in Heaven, will you listen a bit,
I am talking to you from below.
Thare is quite a few things I don't understand,
and a whole lot more I don't know

When I look back over my wild rugged life
and the things I used to do
I could never have lived to be old as I am
if it had not been for you.

I have worked for the Devil the most of my life;
Lord, I made him a hand
but now I've come over to your side of the range
and it was not because I got canned.

I have rode bad horses in three western states
that was plenty mean and tough,
and worked wild cattle in mountain range
that was plenty brushy and rough.

There was many times in life, dear Lord,
the jackpots I was in;
I never dreamed you protected me,
or cared about my sin.

Since I have found you now, dear Lord,
  I know how I got through.
You helped me out in every way—
  all the credit goes to you.

I have pulled many bone heads in my life
  like many old cowboys do,
but I have rode gentle ponies, lived better life
  since I been working for you.

Satan, I reckon, misses me now
  for I could stir up a whole lot of sin.
I never failed him on any job,
  no difference what shape I was in.

But laying all other jokes aside,
  understanding is what I crave.
I don't mind leaving this old body of mine
  down here in a six-foot grave.

My *spirit* is what I am thinking about
  since I am trying to get it clean.
I never cuss or drink any more
  and never think anything mean.

I have cowboy friends that went some place
  and some relations, too;
I pray dear Lord you gathered them in,
  and they are all there with you.

When you get ready to put out my light,
  I pray your favor I have won,
that you will let me hang out at your
  Headquarter Ranch
  when my work on earth is done.

[1]Pecos told this story to me personally. It appeared as "The Branding of a Maverick," in *Decision* magazine, November 1962, pp. 6-7. © 1962, the Billy Graham Evangelistic Association.

[2]The letters appear in *Pecos' Poems,* ed. by Joe Evans and published by Evans and Pecos Higgins in El Paso, TX, 1957.

[3]*Decision* magazine, op.cit.

[4]Joe Evans, *Cowboy Camp Meetings,* self-published by Evans in El Paso, TX, 1965, p. 19.

[5]*Pecos Poems,* op.cit.

[6]This poem, reproduced here in its complete form, is found in Joe Evans' self-published *Ol' Spot, The Lead Steer,* El Paso, 1964, pp. 65-66. Courtesy Wheaton College Archives and Billy Graham Center Archives, Wheaton, IL.

Francis of Assisi

Like music carried by a breeze across the waters from a distant shore, the lilting song of Francis of Assisi comes to us over a span of eight hundred years of time. It is a song of joy, yet it is muted and tempered by medieval cadences that threaten to interrupt its rhythm and cloy its natural sweetness.

Francis was not primarily a man of religion. He was a man of joy who took his joy from Jesus. By doing so he was able to bring a new spirit into medieval Europe, something fresh that conveyed zest and spirit to the worn-out trappings and customs of the ecclesiastical establishment. Francis became the Minstrel of Jesus, the Troubadour of God, the singing Knight Errant of the King of Heaven.

"The Devil rejoices most when he can snatch away any spiritual joy from a servant of God," he declared. "When the soul is wretched and desolate it is easily overwhelmed by its sorrow, or else it turns to idle enjoyments. But when spiritual joy fills the heart, the serpent throws off his deadly poison in vain."[1]

Who was this man for whom San Francisco was named, and for whom an enormous religious order was formed that still touches thousands of lives around the globe? So many have written biographies of him that one shrinks from repeating the facts.[2] He was born in Assisi, an Umbrian town at the foot of Mount Subasio in central Italy, in the year 1182. He died in 1226 at the age of 44.

Francis grew up in a well-to-do family, and prior to his conversion was a popular young man around town. On one fete day he was named "master of the revels." After a brief military venture his life took a different turn and he became deeply pious, thereby causing a family rupture.

Physically Francis' build was slight and his health never truly robust, a condition that was not improved by the rigorous disciplines of his church. After his change of heart Francis' fellow citizens thought his behavior strange, but before long his reputation for genuine holiness began to grow. His winning personality and devotion to his Lord drew other young men, and the Franciscan order of friars, duly sanctioned by the Vatican, began to emerge.

Francis was never a "Pharisaical" or legalistic type, but he was certainly a man of the church. He maintained cordial relationships with his superiors, with his colleague Dominic, the founder of the Dominican order, and other church figures. He attracted huge crowds wherever he spoke, and even obtained a hearing before the Sultan of Egypt in the midst of a siege of war. He had great gifts of leadership, but he became convinced that wealth was a principal cause of evil and corruption in the church. Accordingly he instituted a rule of poverty, and did his best to see that it was followed.

Unfortunately his movement became so popular that it brought affluence with it, and frustration to its founder. Francis' insistence on living a life of simplicity and poverty caused him eventually to resign from his own order, which was then spreading far and wide. It was not, however, his devotion to Lady Poverty that made Francis the most popular figure in Christianity after Christ. Rather it was his unconquerable joy.

Within two years of his death Francis of Assisi was canonized as a saint of his church.

This sketchy background, which perforce must pass up much that others consider important about Francis, is only recorded in order to emphasize this one unique aspect of the man's character and personality. What made Francis so singular in appeal, and so different from religious figures of his day, was his determination to make the devotional life in Christ a life of joyousness and exuberance. To him being a child of God was fun.

One of his earliest biographers says that Francis "made it a point to keep himself in joy of heart and to preserve the unction of the Spirit and the oil of gladness."[3] He told his companions if they felt dejected, they should start praying and stay there until they found the Heavenly Father driving out the "Babylonian stuff" and restoring the joy of His salvation. On one occasion Francis called his followers together specifically to tell them, "Beware lest you show yourselves outwardly gloomy and sad hypocrites. Rather show yourselves joyful in the Lord, cheerful and suitably gracious."[4]

One day, we are told, Francis sought a place of prayer and began to think in bitterness of soul about the wretched years he had spent before giving his life to God. As he kept repeating the words, "God, be merciful to me, a sinner,"[5] little by little a certain unspeakable joy and sweetness flooded his heart. The effect was that he was renewed in spirit and "seemed changed into another man."[6]

Francis' love of nature, of flowers and trees, green gardens and forests, cornfields and vineyards, birds and animals, brought a unique quality to his preaching. He would call the different creatures "brother" and "sister," and applied such endearments even to sun and moon, earth and fire, air and wind. Nature often filled him, we are told, with "a wonderful and ineffable joy."

It is said that Francis would sometimes pick up a stick from the ground and laying it over his left arm, he would draw another stick across it with his right hand like a bow, as though he were playing a violin. Then he would imitate the movements of a musician and sing songs in French about the Lord in an ecstasy of joy.[7] The play instinct was strong with Francis, and proved contagious among his followers.

When he was being treated for trouble with his eyes, Francis once called a companion who had formerly been a lute player. He said to him, "Brother, I would like you to borrow a lute secretly and bring it here so that with it you may give some wholesome comfort to Brother Body [that is, himself] that is so full of pains."

The brother answered him, "I am not a little ashamed to do so, Father, because I am afraid men may suspect that I am being tempted to frivolity."

Francis said, "Let us then forget about it, Brother. It is good to give up many things so that the opinion of others may not be harmed."

His biographer adds that the next night there suddenly came "the sound of a lute of wonderful harmony and very sweet melody. No one was seen, but the volume of the sound marked the going and coming of the lute player as he moved back and forth."[8] Francis thought he had been transported to another world.

On a particular occasion one of Francis' closest companions, Brother Leo, recorded a famous statement of Francis on the subject of joy. A popular version of that statement has been repeated often in a late collection known as "The

Little Flowers of St. Francis."[9] That version is not however the one being presented here, for a good reason. In 1927 a different version was published, taken from a recently uncovered fourteenth century Latin manuscript which has been attributed to Brother Leonard of Assisi, a companion of Francis and Leo. This version, because it is shorter and more realistic, many consider to be earlier and therefore more authentic.

Brother Leonard's version follows:

One day at St. Mary ["of the Angels," an Assisi church], St. Francis called Brother Leo and said, "Brother Leo, write this down."

He answered, "I'm ready."

"Write what true joy is," he said. "A messenger comes and says that all the masters of theology in Paris have joined the [Franciscan] Order—write: that is not true joy. Or all the prelates beyond the mountains—archbishops and bishops, or the King of France and the King of England—write: that is not true joy. Or that my friars have gone to the unbelievers and have converted all of them to the faith; or that I have so much grace from God that I heal the sick and I perform many miracles. I tell you that true joy is not in all those things."

"But what is true joy?" [asked Brother Leo.]

"I am returning from Perugia and I am coming here at night in the dark. It is winter time and wet and muddy and so cold that icicles form at the edges of my habit and keep striking my legs, and blood flows from such wounds. And I come to the gate, all covered with mud and cold and ice, and after I have knocked and called for a long time, a friar comes and asks, 'Who are you?'

"I answer: 'Brother Francis.'

"And he says, 'Go away. This is not a decent time to be going about. You can't come in.'

"And when I insist again, he replies: 'Go away. You are a simple and uneducated fellow. From now on don't stay with us any more. We are so many and so important that we don't need you.'

"But I still stand at the gate and say, 'For the love of God, let me come in tonight.'

"And he answers, 'I won't. Go to the Crosiers' Place and ask there.'

"I tell you that if I kept patience and was not upset—that is true joy and true virtue and the salvation of the soul." [10]

—

Such a definition may appear strange to modern ears, but to one who is familiar with Francis of Assisi's warm spiritual outlook and exciting lifestyle, it fits. Elsewhere Brother Leo is quoted as saying:

> It was always the supreme and particular desire of blessed Francis to possess an abiding joy of spirit outside times of prayer and divine office. This was the virtue that he especially loved to see in his brethren, and he often reproached them when they showed signs of gloom and despondency.[11]

When men were first attracted to his cause, wishing to share the joy in the Spirit that he had discovered, Francis introduced them to renunciation and self-denial. But in describing those early days it would be anachronistic to speak of a "Franciscan Order." The men were not an *order*, they were simply Francis' companions in the faith. They went where he went, or where he told them to go. They lived in no house; they did not even settle in a church. Rather they walked through the countryside looking for work so they could fill the common larder. They helped peasants in the fields, then at night talked to them about Jesus. They slept in barns and haylofts, in lepers' houses, or under the porch of some church.

Barefoot, penniless, thinly clad in patched tunics and shabby drawers, singing and praying and praising the Lord, they were a Spirit-filled band. One biographer speaks of "chaste embraces, gentle feeling, a holy kiss, pleasing conversation, modest laughter, joyous looks, submissive spirits and peaceful tongues." They found much to laugh about. "They came together with great desire; they remained together with joy; but separation from one another was sad on both sides."[12]

If they were cold, they built a fire. If there was no food, they were not above going out and begging for it. If people tried to venerate them, they outsmarted them by such gambits as see-sawing with children. Hardship they welcomed; scandal they avoided. When they were offered money they refused it. Cares and fears, malice and rancor, envy and bitterness and abusive speech were not for them; they were at peace.

For such a congenial fellowship to expand into a worldwide religious order is a story for others to relate. I shall leave our cheerful and charming friends on the Umbrian plain with the "little poor man of Assisi," making the kind of music they loved and reflecting the joys of Heaven. May God bless them, for they have blessed millions.

---

[1] *Omnibus of Sources, Writings and Early Biographies of St. Francis of Assisi,* Marion A. Habig, ed., Chicago, Herald Press, 1983, p. 465 (II Celano 88:125).

[2] My favorite biographer of Francis is Paul Sabatier, the French Protestant scholar whose researches led to a significant change in Franciscan studies. See his *Life of St. Francis of Assisi,* tr. by Louise Houghton, London, Hodder & Stoughton, 1894.

[3] *Omnibus,* op.cit., pp. 465-66 (II Celano 88).

[4] *Omnibus,* op.cit., (II Celano 91).

[5] Luke 18:13.

[6] *Omnibus,* op.cit., p. 156 (I Celano 26).

[7] From *The Mirror of Perfection,* op cit., p. 1226.

[8] From *The Mirror of Perfection,* op.cit.

[9] From *Little Flowers of St. Francis,* Part 1, No. 8, in *Omnibus,* op.cit., p. 1318.

[10] *Omnibus,* op.cit., pp. 1501-02.

[11] *Omnibus,* op.cit., pp. 466-67 (II Celano 89).

[12] *Omnibus,* op.cit., pp. 260-62 (I Celano 38, 39).

Brother Lawrence of the Resurrection

The collection of Brother Lawrence's thoughts and writings, popularly known as *The Practice of the Presence of God,* contains some rare jewels on the subject of joy. In these pages I have attempted to string together those jewels to form a necklace whose beauty the reader can judge. Some are taken from conversations with the Superior of his monastery, Abbé Joseph de Beaufort, and are expressed in the third person. Other excerpts are taken from Brother Lawrence's personal letters to various friends. I have rendered the original French account in a fresh translation, which seeks to follow the precise French wording whenever the English counterpart permits. Several published English translations have also been consulted.

In this excerpt no attempt has been made to follow the usual structure of the book. I have been helped by *The Practice of the Presence of God,* translated by John J. Delaney (New York, Image Books, 1977) and by *La Présence de Dieu dans La Vie de Tous les Jours,* published by Labor et Fides, Geneva, Switzerland, n.d.

Brother Lawrence was a man of bright spirit who loved God and worried about nothing. Born to devout parents early in the 17th century in Herimesnil, Lorraine, France, he was named Nicolas Hermann. Serving in the army of Lorraine in the 30 Years War, he was captured, accused of spying, released and later wounded. That ended his military service. In 1640 he was accepted as a lay brother of the Discalced Carmelites in Paris, and was assigned to the monastery kitchen. Due to lameness he was later transferred to shoe repair. He died at the monastery after a painful illness in 1691.

The Abbé de Beaufort Describes His Visits With Brother Lawrence

The first time that I saw Brother Lawrence, he told me that God had given him singular grace in his conversion, being still in the world at 18 years of age. It happened on a winter day when he saw a tree stripped of its leaves. As he considered the fact that some time later the leaves would appear anew, followed by flowers and fruit, he received a high view of the providence and power of God which has never been effaced from his soul.

This view detached him entirely from the world, and gave him such a love for God that he was not able to say if it had ever been augmented in the more than forty years since he had received this grace.

He said he had been a lackey to Monsieur William de Fieubert, the French national treasurer of savings, and as such he was a great lout who smashed everything. He requested to enter the religious life, believing that he could punish himself there for his faults and clumsy behavior by sacrificing his life and all his pleasures to God. However, God "took him in," for he found nothing but satisfaction in it.

He said that we should give ourselves entirely in a pure

abandonment to God in things both temporal and spiritual, and take our joy in the execution of His will, whether it leads us to suffering or to consolations. They are all the same to him who is truly abandoned.

Material occupations do not divert him from his contemplation. "The times of action are no different from the times of prayer, because I possess God in tranquillity both during the bustle of the kitchen where sometimes many people demand things of me at the same time, and when I am on my knees before the altar. It is not necessary to have great things to do. I turn my little omelet in the frying pan for the love of God; when that is achieved, if I have nothing to do, I prostrate myself on the ground and adore my God from whom has come the grace for me to do it. After that I rise up more contented than a king."

He found it necessary to establish himself in the presence of God by continually talking with him. He considered it disgraceful to interrupt such a conversation in order to deal with a lot of twaddle. Since the soul requires a high concept of God for its own nourishment, and derives great joy from it, we need a revival of our faith. It is pitiful to see how little faith we have. The highway of faith is the breath of the church, and is the route by which we arrive at holiness. But instead of making faith our rule of life, we amuse ourselves with brief devotions that we change every day.

He was not shocked at the miseries and sin he heard about every day; on the contrary, in view of the malice of which sinners are capable, he was surprised there was not more of it. He prayed for such people, but knowing that God could remedy the world's ills whenever He pleased, he troubled himself no further about the matter.

He said in the beginning one ought to form the habit of

conversing continually with God, and reporting to Him everything that one does; but after a little care, one can feel awakened by His love without any anxiety whatever. In difficulties we had only to turn to Jesus Christ and ask for His grace; with that everything becomes easy. His principal concern is to be with God always, to do nothing, say nothing and think nothing that would displease Him, solely for love of Him.

He said it was a great deception to believe that the time of prayer ought to be different from other times. We were strictly obliged to be as united to God by working in the time of work as by praying in the time of prayer. He retired to pray when Father Prior told him to, but he neither desired it nor demanded it, as his hardest work did not distract him from God.

His prayer was nothing more than the presence of God. His soul then put to sleep everything else except love; but afterward he found little difference. He kept himself always close to God, blessing and praising Him with all his might, living his life in a continual joy, yet hoping that God would give him something to suffer when he was a little stronger.

Brother Lawrence said he was always governed by love, without any other interest and without troubling himself as to whether he was damned or saved. But having made the end of all his actions the love of God, he found himself well off. He was content when he could pick up a straw from the ground for the love of God, seeking Him alone purely and nothing else, not even His gifts.

Often, he felt, the ecstasy and rapture that came to him was nothing more than a soul taking pleasure in the gift, instead of bypassing it and going directly to God who is greater than all His gifts. One might be surprised and carried away by such an experience, but God was still the Master. God repaid everything he (Brother Lawrence) did for Him so promptly and munificently that he sometimes wished that he could hide from God what he was trying to do, so that he could have the pleasure of doing something purely for the love of God and without receiving any reward.

In the past he had great pain in his spirit, believing certainly that he was damned, and all the men in the world could not change his opinion. This painful thought caused him a great deal of suffering for four years. He finally reasoned on these things in this manner: "I only came into religion for the love of God. I have nothing to do but work for Him; and whether I am damned or saved, I want always to continue to work purely for the love of God. Until I die I shall do whatever is in my power for love of Him."

After that he saw that his pain came from a lack of faith, and since then he has lived in perfect liberty and continual joy. He placed his sins between God and himself, as if to tell Him that he did not merit His favors, but that did not hinder God from heaping them up.

He said one must make a great difference between the actions of the understanding and those of the will. The former amounted to little, but the latter meant everything. He had only to love and take joy in the love of God.

All the penitences in the world, if they were separated from love, would not serve to efface a single sin. We ought, without anxiety, to expect the pardon of our sins through the blood of Jesus Christ, while working solely to love Him with all our hearts. God seems to choose those who had been the greatest sinners to demonstrate the greatness of His grace, rather than those who dwell in innocence, because they display His goodness to advantage.

He always addressed God when he was presented with some opportunity to practice a virtue, saying to Him, "My Lord, I shall not be able to do this unless You make me able to do it" and immediately, he said, "He gave me the power to do it." Then when he made a mess of it, he did nothing but confess his fault and say to God, "I will never do anything else but fail if You leave it for me to do. Since I am absolutely decided to follow you, it is up to You to keep me from falling and to correct that which is not good." After that he gave himself no trouble about his shortcomings, assured as he was of the pardon of God.

He said it was important for us to behave very simply with God, and to speak to Him plainly and frankly in asking His help in our affairs as they develop. God would not fail to give it, as he himself had often proved.

Even in the kitchen chores, for which he had a great natural aversion, he had accustomed himself to doing everything for the love of God. On every occasion he had asked the Lord for grace to do his work, and had found it very easy to fulfill his tasks during the fifteen years he had been occupied there. He was now in the shoe-repair shop where he was delighted to be, but he was as ready to quit that employment as he had the others. His only wish was to take special joy in doing little things for the love of God.

Many people become switched off (he continued) in penitences and particular exercises while neglecting love, which is the real end. This can be readily seen in their works; and is the reason we see so little solid virtue. Neither finesse nor science is needed to go to God, but only a heart resolved to devote itself to Him and for Him, and to love Him only.

We should feed our souls on lofty thoughts of God, and so take great joy in being with Him. Without being discouraged on account of our sins, and while paying no attention to our feelings, we should pray for His grace in complete confidence, relying on the infinite merits of our Lord Jesus Christ. God, he declared, never fails to offer us His grace for every undertaking.

Excerpts Taken From Brother Lawrence's Own Letters

There is not in the world a life more pleasing and more delicious than a life of continual conversation with God; only those can understand it who practice and experience it. If I were a preacher, I would preach above everything else the practice of the presence of God. If I were a director [pastoral counselor], I would counsel the whole world to do the same, so necessary I believe it to be and at the same time so easy.

I have renounced all special forms of devotion and prayer except those which my position obliges me to fulfill. I strive only to dwell in His holy presence, and do that by a simple attention and loving gaze constantly fixed upon Him, which I am able to call a *real presence* of God; or to say it better, a secret conversation, silent and habitual, of the soul with God. I experience in this way ravishments of inner joy and sometimes such external joys that I am forced to use means to restrain them, for fear that others would not understand them.

To sum up, I have the assurance that my soul has been with God during these past thirty years. Still, I believe it appropriate to inform you in what manner I regard myself before God, whom I regard as my King.

I consider myself the most miserable of men, full of corruption, having committed all sorts of crimes against my

King. Animated by a true repentance, I confess to Him my wickedness, I ask of Him His pardon, and abandon myself into His hands for whatever He is able to do with me and whatever He pleases to do. I beg Him to make me according to His heart. The King, full of goodness and mercy, far from chastising me, embraces me with love, makes me eat at His table, serves me with His own hands, and gives me the key to His treasure. He talks with me steadily in thousands and thousands of ways and treats me with all deference as His beloved. He forgives me and relieves me of my principal bad habits without talking about them. Always the more weak and despicable I see myself to be, the more beloved I am of God.

I do not know how God will dispose of me. I am always happy. The whole world suffers; and I, who merit the most severe discipline, find myself filled with a joy so continual and so grand that I am hardly able to contain it. When I know I have failed, I acknowledge it and say, "That is what I usually do when I am left to myself." If I have not failed, I give thanks to God and acknowledge it is His doing.

The practice of the presence of God strengthens us in our hope; our hope grows in proportion to our knowledge. To the extent that our faith by this holy practice penetrates the mysteries of the divine, to that extent does it discover in God a beauty that surpasses infinitely not only that of the bodies we see on earth, but that of the angels as well. So our hope grows and is strengthened, encouraged and sustained by the grandeur of this good which it desires to enjoy, and that in some way it savors.

Billy Bray

Why would a man leap and dance in the pulpit? Is it because he is glad? Or just mad?

I am speaking of a Cornishman who was born just two hundred years ago to a poor family in an impoverished land. Cornwall is located in the extreme southwestern corner of England. The year was 1794 and the place was Twelveheads, a tiny village with a few thatched-roof houses. From his youth, the lad grew up to make his living digging out ore in a tin mine a thousand feet underground, struggling against frightful working conditions—until he was fired.

As to the grown man, he turned out to be short, wiry, bald-headed, and more often than not (until his thirtieth year) drunk. When he spoke, he fairly fractured the English language with his Cornish vernacular. The account he wrote of his own life betrayed a meager education. Until Jesus Christ entered his life he was, in his own words, a bad-tempered, undisciplined showoff, soaked in gin and desperately poor. Of all the reckless men of the county he was rated the wildest and most daring. His cursing was such that his own drinking companions said, "His oaths must come from hell, for they smell of sulphur."

This was William Trewartha Bray, known even today as Billy Bray, the Glory Man, perhaps the most famous

Cornishman in history.[1] He was a Methodist lay preacher who led thousands of his fellow Cornishmen and women to Jesus Christ until his homegoing in 1868 at age 73. Today people still talk about him—and write books about him.

Why?

Because of his joy.

Billy Bray's conversion took place in 1823 after reading the book, *Visions of Heaven and Hell,* by John Bunyan. Several desperate bouts of prayer took place before Billy laid hold on the promises of God and changed, as he said, "from a mad-man to a glad-man." A few months later he began publicly to exhort people to repent and turn to God. He attended no Bible school or seminary, for they were non-existent in Cornwall. His life, and the lives of his wife and children, depended totally upon his earnings in the tin mine.

The man proved, however, to be a master of communication. Three quarters of a century earlier John Wesley had brought Methodism to Cornwall, giving the hope of the Gospel for the first time to the poor people living in the squalid villages. This was the message Billy Bray heard in the tiny stone chapels of his day. By the end of 1824 his name was put on the Local Preachers' Plan, as it was called. He received no other ordination from men, but the Spirit of God touched him with the ordaining that matters most. Within a few years this lay exhorter's fame had spread all over Cornwall.

Let us pay a visit to one of the Bible chapels where Billy Bray is preaching tonight. It is built of gray granite, unadorned save for the furniture: a plain pulpit, a plainer communion table, and some oak pews. Because it is the Lord's Day the invited guest does not ride to church.

Instead he has walked for several miles. "Does he care to rest now that he has arrived? Is he not tired?"

Billy Bray laughs. "All the way here I just put one foot before the other. And every time I put one foot down I shouted 'Glory,' and every time I put the other down I cried out, 'Hallelujah!' "

The chapel is so full of worshipers that he has difficulty getting in the front door, but as soon as the people hear his peculiar tone of voice saying, "Bless the Lord! Little Billy Bray is come once more to the chapel," passage is made for him.

When he reaches the pulpit Billy begins to dance and shout for joy. He reads the first line of a Charles Wesley hymn,

> O, for a thousand tongues to sing
> the great Redeemer's Name.

Then he pauses and says, "Just think, that's nine hundred and ninety-nine more than I have got! But many of you don't sing with the one tongue you have."

Some object to his antics. "For goodness sake, Billy, do 'ee stop capering about so! Making such to-do is not religion."

To which he replies, "I was born in the fire and cannot live in the smoke. It's not my fault. If a person were to pour water into a basin on a beautiful tablecloth, and the basin was already full, and it was splashing all about, you would not blame the basin. You would tell the person to stop pouring the water. I am only the basin; my Heavenly Father is the one pouring the Water of Life freely, and if you can't bear it, call on Him not to pour so much."

He warms to his subject.

"Why shouldn't I dance as well as David? Don't the Bible mean what's written there? David danced before the Lord with all his might. And not only David the king, neither. All of the house of Israel brought up the ark of the Lord with shouting and the sound of a trumpet. What have 'ee to say to that, then? Are 'ee going to stand alongside Saul's daughter Michal, who looked on David dancing before the Lord and despised him in her heart? If David had something to dance about and leap about because he was bringing back the ark of the Lord to where it did belong, don't *we* have much more to dance and shout about than he did? Why, we've got the Lord Himself! And do you know what we sing, what Wesley wrote with his own hand:

> True treasures abound
> in the rapturous sound
> and my heart it doth dance
> at the sound of His Name.

"If David could dance, and John Wesley could dance, why can't poor Billy Bray dance and shout? It's a poor spectacle when we have nothing but the *telling* part of the love of Christ; it is the *feeling* part that makes us happy. Listen to the Psalm: 'Thou has turned for me my mourning into dancing: Thou hast put off my sackcloth, and girded me with gladness; to the end that my glory may sing praise to Thee, and not be silent. O Lord my God, I will give thanks unto Thee forever.' And listen to Jeremiah: 'Then shall the virgin rejoice in the dance, both young men and old together; for I will turn their mourning into joy, and will comfort them, and make them take joy from their sorrow.'"[2]

By this time the meeting place is filled with joyful noise and frequent uproar, and Billy is at the heart of it. To stay the complaints of those who continue to object to the confusion, he quotes from the celebration at the foundation of the second temple, as recorded in Ezra:

"And all the people shouted with a great shout, and the noise was heard afar off."[3] To those who plead for serenity, Billy adds, "Our blessed Lord has said, 'Ask and ye shall receive, that your joy may be full.' We must have a full joy ourselves to know what a full joy means!"

He tells an anecdote about himself: "I went in to Truro to buy a frock for the little maid [his daughter] and coming home I felt very happy, and got catching up my heels a little bit, and I danced the frock out of the basket. When I came home Joey [his wife] said, "William, where's the frock?"

"I said, 'I don't know, es-en-a in the basket?'

" 'No,' said Joey.

" 'Glory be to God,' I said, 'I danced the frock out of the basket.'

"The next morning I went to the class-meeting, and one was speaking of his trials, and another was speaking of his trials, and I said, 'I've got trials too, for yesterday I went into Truro and bought a frock for the little maid. Coming home I got catching up my heels a little bit and I danced the frock out of the basket.' So they gave me the money I had paid for the frock; and two or three days afterward someone picked up the frock and brought it to me, so I had two frocks for one.[4]

"Glory! If they were to put me into a barrel, I would shout glory out through the bunghole. Praise the Lord! The Devil knows where I live. He do try and get at me when I'm not looking. He's so cunning you got to be on the watch all the time.

" 'I'll have thee down to hell after all, Billy,' the Devil said to me.

" 'Aw, will 'ee now? Hast thee got a little lew [sheltered] place in hell where I could sing thee a song? I'll sing thee a song about Jesus Christ, and shout, and praise the Lord. And that's a sound thee hasn't heard in hell for fourteen years! How would 'ee like that, Devil?' "

At last the service is ended, but now the after-meeting begins, and people are singing and praying and weeping and dancing and shouting. A man calls out that he has found salvation. Billy Bray leaves the pulpit and leaps down to where the man is standing, bends over and lifts him up from his knees and carries him around the chapel in triumph. Though short of stature, Billy has a tin-miner's muscles in his arms and shoulders, and can easily lift a man.

The antics of Billy Bray during a church service may have appeared designed to be theatrical, but they were not. He also danced in the tunnels and stopes of the tin mines, and in the bedroom of his house. When his beloved wife Joey died, Billy was away from home, but he returned to find the cottage filled with mourners. They soon heard his feet beating on the floorboards above them as he shouted, "Glory! My dear Joey is gone up with the bright ones!"[5]

What was the source of all this joy? How could it survive in such an unfavorable environment? Was he always so ecstatic? To the latter question the answer is No. Billy was a human being, and life taught him some hard lessons. Once in a testimony meeting he gave a hint of his unique approach: "Listen, my dear friends, all my life I've had to take vinegar and honey. But praise the Lord, I've had to take the vinegar with a spoon, while He has given the honey with a ladle."

Why would a man dance in the pulpit? There can be only one reason: Because he saw the ineffable glory of God, and felt the love of Heaven come streaming into his own soul by the Holy Spirit. The joy that has bypassed so many philosophers and kings and holy men found its way into the modest cottage of a worn-out Cornish tin miner and lay preacher.

When Billy Bray was nearly seventy-four years old, he lay dying on his bed with his eyes closed. His children, friends and loved ones gathered around his bed, praying. Then Billy opened his eyes for the last time, and spoke one word in his odd native accent:

"Glow—ry!"[6]

---

[1]This extract from the life of Billy Bray is based on the biography by F. W. Bourne, *Billy Bray, The King's Son,* of which over fifty editions have appeared since the 1870s. Bourne, who was a friend of Bray, made extensive use of the "memoranda" that Billy left concerning his life. The edition quoted here was published in 1966 in London by Epworth Press.

In 1979 *The Glory Man: A New Biography of Billy Bray* by Cyril Davey, was published by Hodder & Stoughton, London. This volume provides additional religious, geographical and historical material about the environment in which Billy Bray moved. Also consulted was a chapter on Billy Bray in Anna T. McPherson's book, *Spiritual Secrets of Famous Christians,* published by Zondervan, Grand Rapids, in 1964.

[2]Bourne, op.cit., pp. 37, 45; Davey, op.cit., pp. 67-68.

[3]Ezra 3:11.

[4]Bourne, op.cit., p. 47.

[5]Bourne, op.cit., p. 86.

[6]Davey, op.cit., pp. 134-55.

PART THREE

What Christians Think of Joy

Joy is the most underworked word in the Christian message; yet the New Testament uses it lavishly. The magi had joy when they saw the star over Bethlehem. Joy sent Jesus Christ to the cross. The disciples had joy when they saw the risen Lord. There was great joy in Samaria after Philip preached forgiveness through the cross of Christ. Paul defined the Kingdom of God as joy and the fruit of the Spirit as joy. The New Testament itself was composed in a spirit of joy. Says A. W. Tozer, "The book of Acts is almost hilarious with joy."[1]

The Westminster Shorter Catechism declares that "the chief end of man is to glorify God and enjoy Him forever." Yet Martin Luther remarked that most people have just enough religion to keep them from getting pleasure out of their sin, but not enough to give them any real joy in believing.

Of all the joyous tributes to Jesus outside of Scripture, this one by Arthur John Gossip is my favorite: "There is no growing tired of Christ, no thought of seeking elsewhere for a fuller satisfaction than He gives. Whoso lives with Christ and in Christ has in his heart a spring of water perennial and inexhaustible; a peace that passes understanding; a joy deeper and more real than any other joy; a life far more abundant than anyone else can know; a power that can meet every call upon it—a perpetual fountain, clear and clean, cooling and refreshing."[2]

In the pages that follow the reader will be introduced to a unique company of men and women. These Christians have learned from Jesus that joy is the reflex to love's stimulus. In other words, the Kingdom of God is a Kingdom of love, and joy is an expression of that love. It is hoped that this sampling will evoke more outpourings of joy-filled writing to the glory of God.

—

Words of joy are like sluice gates;
open them and floods pour through.
—Amy Carmichael

WE ARE CHOSEN FOR JOY

by William Barclay

Millions of Christians have read The Daily Study Bible by this distinguished teacher, for many years Lecturer in New Testament Language and Literature at the University of Glasgow, Scotland.

However hard the Christian way is, both in the traveling and in the goal, it is the way of joy. We are chosen for joy. There is always the joy in doing the right thing. When we have evaded some duty or task, and at last we set our hand to it, joy comes to us. The Christian is the man of joy; the Christian is the laughing cavalier of Christ. A gloomy Christian is a contradiction in terms, and nothing in all religious history has done Christianity more harm than its connection with black clothes and long faces. It is true that the Christian is a sinner, but he is a redeemed sinner; and therein lies his joy. How can any person fail to be happy when he or she is walking the ways of life with Jesus?

To be with Jesus is a thing of joy; in the presence of Jesus there is a sheer thrilling effervescence in life. A gloom-encompassed Christianity is an impossibility. The Christian radiance is something which not all the shadows of life can quench.

Far too many people think of Christianity as something which compels them to do all the things they do not want to do and hinders them from doing all the things they do want to do. Laughter has become a sin instead of—as a famous philosopher called it—"a sudden glory."[3]

—

The surest mark of a Christian is not faith, or even love, but joy.

—Samuel M. Shoemaker

CHEERFULNESS

by Charles Haddon Spurgeon

Considered by many the greatest preacher of the Gospel in the 19th Century, Charles Spurgeon drew thousands weekly to his Baptist tabernacle in London, and his lectures to his students are still studied in Bible schools and seminaries around the world.

I commend cheerfulness to all who would win souls; not levity and frothiness, but a genial, happy spirit. A hearty laugh is no more levity than a hearty cry. There are more flies caught with honey than with vinegar, and there will be more souls led to Heaven by a man who wears Heaven in his face than by one who wears Tartarus (a sunless abyss) in his looks. When you speak of Heaven let your face light up. When you speak of hell—well, then your everyday face will do.

There are some brethren who are naturally of a melancholy disposition. They are always very serious, but in them it is not a sign of grace—it is only an indication that their livers are out of order. They never laugh; they think it would be wicked to do so; but they go about the world increasing the misery of humankind, which is dreadful enough without the addition of their unnecessary portion.

Such people evidently imagine that they were predestinated to pour buckets of cold water upon all human mirth and joy. An individual who has no geniality about him had better be an undertaker, and bury the dead, for he will never succeed in influencing the living. Lazarus is not called out of his grave by sepulchral tones [or] hollow moans.[4]

The opposite of joy is not sorrow. It is unbelief.

—Leslie Weatherhead.

WHAT IS MY GOD?

by Augustine of Hippo

These two classic passages are taken from Augustine's Confessions, which he wrote in 400 A.D. soon after being elected a bishop in north Africa.

I love you, Lord, not doubtingly, but with absolute certainty... And what do I love when I love you?... There is a kind of light, and a kind of melody, and a kind of fragrance, and a kind of food, and a kind of embracing, when I love my God. They are the kind of light and sound and odor and food and love that affect the senses of my inner man. There is another dimension of life in which my soul reflects a light that space itself cannot contain. It hears melodies that never fade with time. It inhales lovely scents that are not blown away by the wind. It eats without diminishing the supply. It never gets separated from the embrace of God and never gets tired of it. That is what I love when I love my God.

—

Who are you, really? Who if not the Lord God?... You are unchanging, and yet you change everything. You are never new, never old; yet you make all things new. You humiliate the proud without their knowing it. You are always active, always resting; gathering, yet needing nothing; bearing, filling, protecting, creating, nourishing, perfecting, seeking what you don't need. You love without getting involved in passion. You are jealous, yet you remain unconcerned. You repent, but without being sorry. You become angry, yet you stay serene. You change your operations but never your plans. You recover what you did not lose in the first place. Never in want, you take joy in what you have won. Never greedy, you exact regular interest. Men will spend their last dime to get you under obligation to them; yet who has anything that is not yours to begin with? You pay debts where you owe nothing, and when you forgive debts you lose nothing.[5]

—

> If you have no joy in your religion, there's a leak in your Christianity somewhere.
>
> —Billy Sunday

THE GRACE OF HAPPY-HEARTEDNESS

by George H. Morrison

There are few graces which the world admires so much as the grace of happy-heartedness. There is a certain perennial attraction in men and women who bear their burdens well. When we see a face all lined with care it often touches the chord of pity in us. We are moved to compassion when it flashes on us what a story is engraven there. But the face that really helps us in our journey is seldom the face of battle and of agony; it is the face which has its sunshine still.

We recognize by an unerring instinct that in happy-heartedness there is a kind of victory. And so we love it as we love the sunshine or the song of the birds upon the summer morning. It takes its place with these good gifts of God.

Think of courage—do we not regard that as a gift? And yet this courage, which with perfect justice we are in the way of regarding as temperamental, is viewed in Scripture as something to be won. Take joy. Are we the masters of our joy? Is not the capacity for joy inherent? Are there not those who gravitate to joy as there are others who gravitate to gloom? And yet our Savior says to His disciples, "These things have I spoken to you that in me you might have joy." And the fruit of the Spirit is love and joy and peace.

Well, now as it is with these, so I take it is with happy-heartedness. In the eyes of God and in the light of Scripture it is a shining virtue to be won. Happy-heartedness is possible for all and the unfailing secret of it lies in the casting of the burden on the Lord.[6]

> The Christian life that is joyless is a discredit to God and a disgrace to itself.
>
> —Maltbie D. Babcock

THE WORK OF THE SPIRIT

by Martin Luther

This passage is taken from Luther's preface to Paul's Letter to the Romans. When John Wesley heard it read in Aldersgate chapel in 1738 A.D., he felt his heart "strangely warmed."

Where the good is not done freely and joyfully, the heart itself is not set on doing God's law.... To fulfill the law we must joyfully and lovingly do its works. We are to live a good life, a godly life, freely and without the law's compulsion; as if, in fact, there were neither law nor punishment.

But this joy, this free and voluntary love, is put into the heart by the Holy Spirit (Romans 5:5). And the Holy Spirit is not given except in, with and through faith in Jesus Christ, as Paul says. Faith, in turn, does not come except through the Word of God, or the Evangel. This Gospel proclaims Christ to be the Son of God, and the One who died and rose again for our sakes.

Thus it comes about that faith alone justifies a man and fulfills the law, for faith brings the Holy Spirit through the merits of Christ. The Spirit makes a man's heart merry and free, as the law demands; so good works proceed out of faith.... Oh, it is a living, creative, active, mighty thing, this faith!... Faith is a daring confidence in God's grace, so sure that it would die a thousand times for it. Such confidence and such knowledge of God's grace makes a person joyous, gay, bold and merry toward God and all creatures. That is what the Holy Spirit does in faith.[7]

—

Joy is distinctly a Christian word and a Christian thing. It is the reverse of happiness. Happiness is the result of what happens of an agreeable sort. Joy has its spring deep down inside, and that spring never runs dry no matter what happens. Only Jesus gives that joy. He had joy, singing its music within, even under the shadow of the cross. It is an unknown word and thing except as He has sway within.

—Samuel Dickey Gordon[8]

A SUFFUSION OF JOY

by Madame Chiang Kai-Shek (Meiling Soong Chiang)

Madame Chiang wrote this testimony in Taipei, Taiwan, where she lived with her husband, the president of the Republic of China, after they fled from Communist armies during the winter of 1949-50.

Soon after my arrival in Taiwan I invited five of my friends who were devout Christians to our home and told them that from that day forth I hoped to have a prayer group. A prayer group is nothing new, but with this group I experienced what I had so often heard about and never quite understood: spiritual joy and exhilaration.

Very soon I realized that others were feeling the same. This is the fruit of a prayer group: intellectual conviction in the proofs all around them of the power of prayer, plus an entirely fresh suffusion of inward joy. Here is the key to one of the swiftest ways in which faith becomes truly personal.

I had been a nominal Christian. In my mind I accepted unquestionably and unreservedly the divinity of Christ, His teachings and His grace. Then one day while reading of the crucifixion, I wept. At last I felt the suffering and pain of Jesus Christ were for me. I cried and cried, overcome with my own unworthiness. It was a peculiar situation, at once great grief and great release. My tears were a torrent, and at the same time my heart felt light and relieved, with a sense of Christ's atonement.

I think I experienced what is called an old-fashioned conversion. No other word will do. Conversion is very difficult to explain—except to those who have been through it.[9]

—

To miss the joy is to miss all.
—Robert Louis Stevenson

EXPECT GREAT THINGS FROM GOD

by James S. Stewart

Professor Stewart was pastor of North Morningside Church, Edinburgh, Scotland, for many years before joining the University of Edinburgh faculty as New Testament instructor. I was his pupil during the years 1949-1951.

Turn to the New Testament and you find all is freshness and wonder, and a strange eager tension of expectancy, and the continual surprise of discovery. These men indeed had behind them a mighty experience and a memorable hour. But they were not living in a past however sacred. Had not Jesus promised, "Greater things than these you will see?" Had not God declared, "I have glorified My name, and will glorify it again?"

And was not this the thrill, the inexpressible excitement, of being alive in the same world with the risen Christ—that you had to keep your eyes open and your soul on tiptoe, for at any moment some new startling discovery might come breaking in, some fresh unheard-of revelation to leave you lost in wonder, love and praise? The whole church was then expecting great things from God.

The most urgent necessity today is to start taking seriously the good news of the Holy Spirit indwelling the church with power and glory, so that while the church thanks God for all the ways in which He has appeared, far more it reaches out toward the future, realizing that there are signs and wonders still, that still Christ is stronger than the enemy, and that where sin abounds grace much more abounds, and that still across this darkened earth there rings the music of the redeemed, *the new colossal chorus of the morning stars singing together and the sons of God shouting for joy.* It is this that differentiates a dynamic infectious faith from the dull tedium of conventional religion. "I have both glorified My name, and will glorify it again." This is the word of the Lord for you.[10]

—

> We can do nothing well without joy, and a good conscience which is the ground of joy.
>
> —Richard Sibbes

THE GOD-SHAPED VACUUM

by Blaise Pascal

One of the most brilliant scientific minds of any age, Pascal discovered "Pascal's law" of hydraulics and invented the barometer and the calculator, the latter being the forerunner of the computer. He was persecuted by the Inquisition, but never left the Roman Catholic church. He died at 39, while compiling notes (*Pensées*) for a Christian book.

All human beings seek happiness. This is without exception. Whatever means they use, everyone tends toward this end. Some go to war, others don't, but all have the same desire in view. The human will never takes the least step except toward this object. It is the motive of every action of every human being, even of those who hang themselves.

Yet without faith no one ever reaches the goal of happiness toward which we all aspire, even after years of trying. Everybody complains; princes and subjects, noblemen and commoners, old and young, strong and weak, learned and ignorant, health and sick, people of all countries, of all times and ages, and of all conditions. Surely such a mass of evidence, gathered over so long a time, should convince us of our inability to reach the good life by our own efforts. Yet example seems to teach us little, and experience dupes us and leads us from one misfortune to another, and finally to death.

What then do this desire and this inability proclaim to

us? That there was once in man a true happiness, of which there now remains to him only an empty trace which he vainly tries to fill out of his environment. He seeks from things absent the help he cannot obtain from things present. Yet all these efforts are inadequate, because the infinite abyss can be filled only by an infinite and immutable object, that is, by God Himself.[11]

—

> Joy is not gush; joy is not jolliness. Joy is perfect acquiescence in God's will because the soul delights itself in God Himself.
>
> —H. W. Webb-Peploe

The Name of the Samaritan

Adapted from a story by Henry Durbanville

Jean Frédéric Oberlin, from whom Oberlin, Ohio, takes its name, was a Lutheran minister, born in Alsace. He studied theology at Strasbourg and became pastor of a poverty-stricken village in the Vosges mountains, where he turned philanthropist and social reformer, building roads, forming a kindergarten, bringing seeds from the Caucasus to improve agriculture, and starting a savings and loan association. Protestants and Catholics alike attended his services. He died in 1826.

One day Pastor Oberlin was making a winter journey from Strasbourg to his village. Halfway there he was so exhausted struggling through the snow on impassable roads that he commended himself to God. Then he collapsed and fell asleep in the road. After awhile he became conscious of someone rousing him and opened his eyes. Before him stood a wagon driver. With food and drink, Oberlin's vital signs returned and the driver carried him on his wagon to the next village.

There a joyous Oberlin became profuse in his thanks and offered the man money, but it was refused. "It is only a duty to help one another," said the wagoner. He added, "It is the next thing to an insult to offer a reward for such a service."

"Then," said Oberlin, "at least tell me your name, that I may have you in thankful remembrance."

"I see you are a minister of the Gospel," said the wagoner. "Please tell me the name of the good Samaritan." Oberlin said he could not, as Scripture did not reveal it. "Then," said the man, "until you can tell me his name, permit me to withhold mine."[12]

—

The very society of joy redoubles it.

—Robert South

HOW MUCH DO YOU LOVE?

by H. A. Ironside

There is a story about the wife of one of King Cyrus' generals who was charged with treachery against the king. She was called before Cyrus after being tried and sentenced to die. Her husband, who did not realize what had taken place, was apprised of it and came hurrying in. When he heard that the sentence condemned his wife to death, the general threw himself prostrate before the king and said, "O Sire, take my life instead of hers. Let me die in her place!" King Cyrus was so touched that he said, "Love like that must not be spoiled by death." He gave them back to each other and let the wife go free.

As they walked joyfully away the husband said, "Did you notice how kindly the king looked upon us when he gave you a free pardon?"

"I had no eyes for the king," she said. "I saw only the man who was willing to die for me."[13]

> The sort of contagious joy that flows from the laughter of faith is the best guarantee of effective ecclesiastical ministry that can possibly exist.
>
> —Andrew Greeley

RESURRECTION JOY

by Carl F. H. Henry

What significance has the resurrection of Jesus of Nazareth from the dead for us today? I have met worldwide a fellowship of joyous persons whose outlook and character are shaped by the reality and power of Christ's resurrection, and who now have special access to the Risen One. They are men and women who take joy in the redemption and the renewal Christ offers, a company of believers of every race and color on every continent and of every walk of life. All have this in common: whereas like Saul of Tarsus they were once unbelievers who considered Christians a strange lot even if they did not openly persecute them, now like C. S. Lewis they declare themselves "surprised by joy," a matchless, incomparable joy.

The life of the Spirit has a new dynamic through the resurrection and Pentecost. The redeemed enjoy in this life a spiritual and moral union with the exalted Redeemer. "Spirits of antiquity," wrote Bishop Herbert Henson, "have dwelt frequently on the note of despondency, even of despair [in early times]. Against this background of diffused and dominant pessimism, the profession of Christianity presented an arresting spectacle of jubilant hope. The secret of the difference lay in the Christian belief that by His resurrection Christ had validated the human effort." Christian morality has about it an element of buoyant Easter joy sustained by the risen Jesus as our eternal Contemporary.[14]

—

From silly devotions and sour-faced saints,
deliver us, O Lord.

—Teresa of Avila.

SOOTHING STREAMS OF JOY

by a Russian Peasant

In his book, *Christ in the Silence,* C. F. Andrews, missionary to India, quotes "the simple utterance of a Russian peasant pilgrim who did not even place his name on the manuscript he left behind with an old monk of Mount Athos [Greece], so little did he think of himself and so much of Christ." The man's manuscript read:

Prayer has brought me ever-increasing joy, so that many times my heart overflowed with a measureless love for Jesus Christ; and from this sweet spring soothing streams poured through all my bones. The memory of Jesus Christ was so stamped upon my mind that I felt a joy that cannot be expressed. It sometimes happened that for three days and nights I entered no human habitation, and I felt a thrill as though I were alone on earth, alone, an abandoned sinner before the face of a merciful and benevolent God.[15]

Norman Morrison, a Minnesota Bible teacher, tells the story of a turn-of-century evangelist named H. B. Gibbud whose wife found herself with a bare pantry. She learned that her husband had no money. She then summoned him to the kitchen, where he found she had placed an empty flour barrel in the middle of the floor.

"I've heard you say," she informed him, "that if someone

really believed what God said, he could put his head in an empty flour barrel and sing 'Praise God from whom all blessings flow.' Well, Reverend, here's your chance to practice what you preach." The challenge was inescapable, and Mr. Gibbud consented on one condition: that she join him. She agreed, and together they put their heads in the barrel and sang the Doxology.

No one knew what they had done, but the next day, to their joy and amazement, a grocery clerk drove his team to their door with a fresh barrel of flour. The generous donor was never disclosed.

—

Joy is the echo of God's life within us.

—Joseph Marmion

A CONQUERING, NEW-BORN JOY

by William G. Morrice

Maurice Jones sums up the situation in the ancient world: "It was a world where the burden of sin and of human misery was intensely realized, and at no period of his history did man express more clearly his need of redemption. . . ."

Into this old world came "good tidings of great joy"; and what Julius Caesar could not do, what the Stoics, the Epicureans, and the mystery religions had all failed to do, Jesus Christ did. There came into the world with His birth a new spirit that changed all things and gave to men and women the possibility of victory over fear and dejection. The joy that was one of the main characteristics of the new faith eventually swept over the world and captured it for Christ. . . .

The New Testament is the most joyful book in the world. Present day Christians must be recalled to what Matthew Arnold has called that "conquering, new-born joy" that broke into the world with the birth of Jesus Christ and "filled her life with day."[16]

[1]A. W. Tozer, *Paths to Power,* Harrisburg, PA, Christian Publications, n.d., p. 36.

[2]From *The Interpreter's Bible,* Vol. 8, p. 524. ©1980 by Abingdon Press, Nashville. Used by permission.

[3]William Barclay, *The Gospel of John,* Vol. 2, Edinburgh, Saint Andrew Press, 1961, pp. 206-07; *The Gospel of Matthew, idem.*, 1962, 343. Used by permission.

[4]Charles Spurgeon, *The Soul Winner,* Grand Rapids, Eerdmans, 1985, p. 82; quoted in W. Barclay, *The Gospel of John,* Vol. 1, Edinburgh, Saint Andrew Press, 1963, p. 85. By permission.

[5]Augustine, *Confessions,* tr. by S. E. Wirt as *Love Song,* New York, Harper & Row, 1971, pp. 3, 124.

[6]George H. Morrison, *The Afterglow of God,* London, Hodder & Stoughton, 1912, pp. 320-25. Courtesy of the publisher.

[7]Martin Luther, in "The Faith of the Heart," *Decision* magazine, May, 1961, p. 12. © 1961, the Billy Graham Evangelistic Association.

[8]S. D. Gordon, quoted in Frank S. Mead, *Encyclopedia of Religious Quotations,* Westwood, N.J., Fleming H. Revell, p. 258.

[9]Madame Chiang Kai-Shek (Meiling Soong Chiang), in "A Suffusion of Joy," *Decision* magazine, March, 1963, p. 4. © 1963, the Billy Graham Evangelistic Association.

[10]James S. Stewart, *River of Life,* pp. 138-39. © 1972 by James S. Stewart. Excerpted by permission of the publisher, Nashville, Abingdon Press, 1972.

[11]Blaise Pascal, "Pensées," No. 425, in *Spiritual Disciplines* (S. E. Wirt, ed.). © Crossway Books, 1983, p. 13. By permission of Good News Publishers, Wheaton, IL.

[12]Henry Durbanville, *Winsome Christianity,* Edinburgh, B. McCall Barbour, 1969, pp. 47-48.

[13]H. A. Ironside, in "How Much Do You Love?" *Decision* Magazine, May, 1961, p. 2. © 1961, the Billy Graham Evangelistic Association.

[14]Carl F. H. Henry, "The Significance of the Resurrection," in *Spiritual Witness,* (S. E. Wirt, ed.). © Crossway Books, 1991, pp. 191-206. By permission of Good News Publishers, Wheaton, IL.

[15]C. F. Andrews, *Christ in the Silence,* London, Hodder & Stoughton, 1933, p. 215.

[16]William Morrice, *Joy in the New Testament,* Carlisle, U.K., Paternoster Press, 1985, pp. 13-15. Used by permission.

PART FOUR

Laughter Through The Ages

It is the heart that is unsure of its God that is afraid to laugh.

—George MacDonald

What is laughter? The French philosopher Henri Bergson, in his monograph *De Rire* (*On Laughter*), wrote that laughter "is the perception of the substitution of mere mechanism for adaptive pliancy." That's enough to make Heaven laugh.

Where did laughter come from? We know it didn't come from a purring cat or tail-wagging dog, or from a fossil, or a chance combination of chemicals, or a computer simulation. It came as a gift from God, and we ought to thank Him every day for it. As the *Encyclopedia Britannica* says, it "beguiles the present"; that is, laughter charms and diverts the present as hope helps us to face the future.

Mary Webb wrote, "The greatest saints are the merriest-hearted people." An old Shaker philosopher, Brother Calvin Fairchild, put it this way: "Some people think it vulgar to laugh, but let such stand in life's gloomy shadows if they choose. As a general rule the best men and women laugh the most. Good, round, hearty, side-shaking laughter is healthy for everybody."

Even our doctors tell us that laughter benefits the lungs! Have you found something to laugh about today? Some rare treasures lie ahead. Read on . . . .

Classic 17th Century Christian Humor

Good Thoughts in Bad Times

by Thomas Fuller

The Reverend Thomas Fuller, D.D. (1608-1661) was one of England's most popular preachers. His wit and wisdom drew such London crowds to the Chapel of St. Mary Savoy on the Strand that they filled the windows, the sextonry, and the chapel yard. Dr. Fuller's quaint Elizabethan language has been modernized somewhat; otherwise the text is unchanged. The reader can judge for himself or herself whether, during the seventeenth-century national trauma of civil war, this man's life was motivated not only by a deep love for his God and Savior, but also by a light and joyful spirit.[1]

—

Lord, my voice by nature is harsh and untunable, and it is vain to lavish any art to better it. Can my singing of psalms be pleasing to Your ears, which is unpleasant to my own? Yet though I cannot chant with the nightingale, or chirp with the blackbird, I would rather chatter with the swallow, yes, rather croak with the raven, than be altogether silent. Had You given me a better voice, I would have praised You with a better voice. Now what my music lacks in sweetness, let it have in sense, singing praises with understanding. Lord, create in me a new heart, therein to make melody, and I will be contented with my old voice, until in Your due time, being admitted into the choir of heaven, I will have another more harmonious voice bestowed upon me.

—

How easy is pen and paper piety for one to write religiously! I will not say it costs nothing, but it is far cheaper to work one's head than one's heart to goodness. Some, perhaps, may guess me to be good by my writings, and so I shall deceive my reader. But if I do not desire to be good, I most of all deceive myself. I can make a hundred meditations sooner than subdue the least sin in my soul. I was once of a mind never to write any more, for fear that at the last day my writings prove to be records against me. And yet why should I not write? By reading my own book, the disproportion between my lines and my life may make me blush myself (if not into goodness) into less badness than I would do otherwise. That way my writings may condemn me and make me condemn myself, so that God may be moved to acquit me.

—

Lord, this day I disputed with myself, whether or not I had said my prayers this morning, and I could not call to mind any remarkable message from which I could certainly conclude that I had offered my prayers to You. Frozen affections, which left no spark of remembrance behind them! Yet at last I barely recovered one token from which I was assured that I had said my prayers. It seems I had said them, and *only* said them, rather by heart than with my heart. Can I hope that You would remember my prayers, when I had almost forgotten that I had prayed? Or rather have I not cause to fear that You remember my prayers too well, to punish the coldness and badness of them? Alas! Are not devotions thus done so in effect, left undone? Jacob advised his sons at their second going into Egypt, Take double money in your hands; peradventure it was an oversight.[2] So, Lord, I come with my second morning sacrifice: be pleased to accept it, which I desire and endeavor to present with a little better devotion than I did the former.

Lord, I find the genealogy of my Savior strangely checkered with four remarkable changes in four immediate generations.

1. Rehoboam begat Abia; that is, a bad father begat a bad son.
2. Abia begat Asa; that is, a bad father a good son.
3. Asa begat Jehoshaphat; that is, a good father a good son.
4. Jehoshaphat begat Joram; that is, a good father a bad son.[3]

I see, Lord, from this, that my father's piety cannot be inherited; that is bad news for me. But I see also that actual impiety is not always hereditary; that is good news for my son.

Lord, the preacher this morning came home to my heart. A left-handed Gibeonite with his sling did not hit the mark more surely than he hit my darling sins.[4] I could find no fault with his sermon, except that it had too much truth. But this I quarreled at, that he went far from his text to come close to me, and so was faulty himself in telling me of my faults. Thus they will creep out at small crannies who have a mind to escape; and yet I cannot deny that when he spoke (though nothing to that portion of Scripture which he had for his text) was according to the proportion of Scripture. And is not Your Word in general the text at large of every preacher? Yes, I should rather have concluded that if he went from his text, Your goodness sent him to meet me; for without Your guidance it would have been impossible for him so truly to have traced the intricate turnings of my deceitful heart.

—

Lord, I confess this morning I remembered my breakfast, but forgot my prayers. And as I returned no praise, so You might justly have afforded me no protection. Yet You have carefully kept me to the middle of this day, entrusting me with a new debt before I have paid the old score. It is now noon, too late for a morning, too soon for an evening sacrifice. My corrupt heart prompts me to put off my prayers till night; but I know it too well, or rather too ill to trust it. I fear if I defer them till night, at night I shall forget them. Be pleased, therefore, now to accept them. Lord, let not a few hours the later make a breach, especially seeing (be it spoken not to excuse my negligence, but to implore Your pardon) a thousand years in Your sight are but as yesterday. I promise hereafter, by Your assistance, to bring forth fruit in due season. See how I am ashamed the sun should shine on me, now newly starting in the race of my devotions, when he like a giant has run more than half his course in the heavens.

Lord, I discover an arrant laziness in my soul. For when I read a chapter in the Bible, before I begin it, I look to see where it ends. And if it ends not on the same side, I cannot keep my hands from turning over the leaf, to measure the length thereof on the other side. If it swells to many verses, I begin to grudge. Surely my heart is not rightly affected. Were I truly hungry after heavenly food, I would not complain of meat. Scourge, Lord, this laziness out of my soul; make the reading of Your word not a penance, but a pleasure to me. Teach me that as among many heaps of gold, all being equally pure, that heap is the best which is the biggest, so I may esteem that chapter in Your Word the best that is the longest.

Lord, how come wicked thoughts to perplex me in my prayers, when I desire and endeavor only to attend Your service? Now I perceive the cause: at other times I have willingly entertained them, and now they entertain themselves against my will. I acknowledge Your justice, that what formerly I invited, now I cannot expel. Give me hereafter always to bolt out such ill guests. The best way to be rid of such bad thoughts in my prayers is not to receive them out of my prayers.

The Roman senators conspired against Julius Caesar to kill him. That very next morning Artemidorus, Caesar's friend, delivered him a paper (desiring him to peruse it) wherein the whole plot was discovered. But Caesar complimented his life away, being so taken up to return the salutations of such people as met him in the way, that he pocketed the paper, among other petitions, as unconcerned therein and so, going to the senate-house, was slain. The world, flesh and devil have a design for the destruction of men. We ministers bring our people a letter, God's Word, wherein all the conspiracy is revealed. But "who hath believed our report?"[5] Most men are so busy about worldly delights, they are not at leisure to listen to us, or read the letter; but thus, alas! run headlong to their own ruin and destruction.

The poets fable that this was one of the labors imposed on Hercules, to make clean the Augean stable. For therein, they said, were kept 3,000 cattle, and it had not been cleansed for thirty years. But Hercules, by letting the river Alpheus into it, did that with ease which before was conceived impossible. This stable is the pure emblem of my impure soul, which has been defiled with millions of sins for more than thirty years together. O that I might by a lively faith and unfeigned repentance let the stream of that fountain into my soul, which is opened for Judah and Jerusalem.[6] It is impossible by all my pains to purge out my uncleanness, which is quickly done by the rivulet of the blood of my Savior.

In the year of our Lord 1606 there happened a sad overflowing of the Severn Sea on both sides, which some alive do remember. An account was written to John Stow, the chronicler, by Dr. Still, then bishop of Bath and Wells, with three other gentlemen, to insert in his history. One passage of the account I cannot omit: "Among other things of note, it happened that upon the tops of some hills, divers beasts of contrary nature had got up for their safety: dogs, cats, foxes, hares, conies, moles, mice and rats, who remained together very peaceably, without any manner or sign of fear of violence one toward another." How much of man was there then in brute creatures? How much of brutishness is there now in men? Is this a time for those who are sinking for the same cause to quarrel and fall out? In the words of the apostle, "Consider what I say, and the Lord give you understanding in all things."[7]

—

A minister of these times sharply chided one of his parish for having an [illegitimate] child, and told him that he must take orders for the keeping thereof [that is, place the baby in orphanage and pay for its support]. "Why, sir," answered the man, "I conceive it more reasonable that you should maintain it. For I am not book learned, and cannot read not a letter in the Bible; indeed, I have been your parishioner these seven years, present every Lord's day at the church. Yet never did I hear you read the Ten Commandments. I never heard that precept read, 'You shall not commit adultery.'[8] Probably, had you told me my duty, I would not have committed this folly."

—

A careless maid who attended a gentleman's child fell asleep while the rest of the family were at church. A monkey, taking the child out of the cradle, carried it to the roof of the house, and there fell a-dancing and dandling thereof, down head, up heels, as it happened.

The father of the child, returning with the family from the church, commented with his own eyes on his child's sad condition. Bemoan he might, help it he could not. Dangerous to shoot the ape where the bullet might hit the babe. All fall to their prayers as their last and best refuge, that the innocent child might be preserved. But when the ape was well wearied with its own activity it fairly went down and formally laid the child where it was found, in the cradle.

Fanatics have pleased their fancies these late years with turning and tossing and tumbling of Christianity, upward and downward and backward and forward. They have cast and contrived it into a hundred antic postures of their own imagining. It is now to be hoped that after they have tired themselves out with doing of nothing, but only trying and tampering to no purpose, they may at last return and leave Christianity in the same condition wherein they found it.

—

I saw a mother threatening to punish her little child for not rightly pronouncing that petition in the Lord's prayer: "And forgive us our trespasses, as we forgive them that trespass against us."[9] The child essayed as well as it could to utter it, adventuring at "tepasses" and "trepasses" but could not pronounce it aright. It is a shibboleth to a child's tongue, as there is a confluence of hard consonants together. If the mother had punished defect in the child for default, she deserved to have been punished herself, the more so because what the child could not pronounce her parent did not practice. Oh, how lispingly and imperfectly do we say, "As we forgive them that trespass against us!"

---

[1]These selections were taken from Fuller's writings which were published in Exeter, England, between 1645 and 1660. They were republished under his name as *Good Thoughts in Bad Times* by Ticknor and Fields, Boston, 1863.

[2]Genesis 43:12.

[3]1 Kings 14:31; 1 Kings 15:8; 2 Chronicles 17:1; 2 Chronicles 21:1.

[4]Judges 20:16.

[5]Isaiah 53:1.

[6]Ezekiel 47:1-12; Revelation 22:1-2.

[7]2 Timothy 2:7.

[8]Exodus 20:14.

[9]Matthew 6:12.

Classic 18th Century Christian Humor

The Vicar of Wakefield

by Oliver Goldsmith

How odd it will appear to some, perhaps, that a selection from the writings of Oliver Goldsmith (1728-1774) should be chosen to illustrate eighteenth century Christian humor! While Goldsmith studied theology, he never pastored. He also studied medicine, yet never really practiced. He wrote charmingly about ladies, yet never married.

My desire is neither to defend nor to pass judgment. Oliver Goldsmith died early at 47, but he remains one of the great English writers and is still popular today. This excerpt is lifted from his classic novel, *The Vicar of Wakefield,*[1] a work replete with Christian values and good humor. One literary critic classes its theme with the Book of Job: A good and innocent man remains steadfast in his faith and courage when disaster strikes. But we should let Dr. Primrose, the vicar, speak for himself. Read on!

—

I had scarce taken orders a year [as a minister] before I began to think seriously of matrimony. I chose my wife as she did her wedding gown, not for a fine glossy surface, but for such qualities as would wear well. To do her justice, she was a good-natured, notable woman; and as for breeding, there were few country ladies who could show more. She could read any English book without much spellings; but for pickling, preserving, and cookery none could excel her. She prided herself also upon being an excellent contriver in housekeeping; though I could never find that we grew richer with all her contrivances.

However, we loved each other tenderly, and our fondness increased as we grew old. There was, in fact, nothing that could make us angry with the world or each other. We had an elegant house, situated in a fine country, and a good neighborhood. The year was spent in moral or rural amusement, in visiting our rich neighbors, and relieving such as were poor. We had no revolutions to fear, nor fatigues to undergo; all our adventures were by the fireside; and all our migrations from the blue bed to the brown.

As we lived near the road, we often had the traveler or stranger visit us to taste our gooseberry-wine, for which we had great reputation; and I profess that I never knew one of them [to] find fault with it.

Thus we lived several years in a state of much happiness, not but that we sometimes had those little rubs which Providence sends to enhance the value of favors [received]. My orchard was often robbed by schoolboys, and my wife's custards plundered by the cats or the children. The Squire would sometimes fall asleep in the most pathetic parts of my sermon, or his lady return my wife's civilities at church with a mutilated courtesy. But we soon got over the uneasiness caused by such accidents, and usually in three or four days began to wonder how they vexed us.

My children were educated without softness, so they were at once well-formed and healthy; my sons hardy and active, my daughters beautiful and blooming. When I stood in the midst of the little circle, which promised to be the supports of my declining age, I could not avoid repeating the famous story of Count Abensberg, who in Henry II's progress through Germany, while other courtiers came with their treasures, brought his thirty-two children and presented them to his sovereign as the most valuable offering he had to bestow.

[This happy idyll comes to a jarring halt as the vicar learns that his financial fortune is lost and the family is now destitute. He is offered, and accepts, a smaller parish at Wakefield that pays but 15 pounds a year. However, it does include a small house and 20 acres of farmland, which he plans to work. The vicar quietly accepts the fact that he is now a poor man. He sends his son George off to London with five guineas and a Bible verse. The rest of the family finds it difficult to adjust to straitened means.—ed]

The little republic to which I gave laws was regulated in the following manner: By sunrise we all assembled in our common apartment; the fire being previously kindled by the servant. After we had saluted each other with proper ceremony, for I always thought fit to keep up some mechanical forms of good breeding, without which freedom ever destroys friendship, we all bent in gratitude to that Being who gave us another day.

That duty being performed, my son [Moses] and I went to pursue our industry abroad [that is, in the fields] while my wife and daughters employed themselves in providing breakfast, which was always ready at a certain time. I allowed half an hour for this meal, and an hour for dinner, which time was taken up in innocent mirth between my wife and daughters, and in philosophical arguments between my son and me.

When Sunday came, it was indeed a day of finery, which all my sumptuary edicts could not restrain. How well soever I fancied my lectures against pride had conquered the vanity of my daughters; yet I still found them secretly attached to all their former finery; they still loved laces, ribbands, bugles and catgut; my wife herself retained a passion for her crimson paduasoy, because I formerly happened to say it became her.

The first Sunday their behavior served to mortify me. I had desired my girls the preceding night to be dressed early the next day; for I always loved to be at church a good while before the rest of the congregation.

They punctually obeyed my directions; but when we were to assemble in the morning at breakfast, down came my wife and daughters, dressed out in all their former splendor: their hair plastered up with pomatum, their faces patched to taste, their trains trundled up in a heap behind, and rustling at every motion. I could not help smiling at their vanity, particularly that of my wife, from whom I expected more discretion.

In this exigence, therefore, my only resource was to order my son, with an important air, to call our coach. The girls were amazed at the command, but I repeated it with more solemnity than before.

"Surely, my dear, you jest," cried my wife, "we can walk it perfectly well. We want no coach to carry us now."

"You mistake, child," returned I, "we do want a coach; for

if we walk to church in this trim, the very children in the parish will hoot after us."

"Indeed," replied my wife. "I always imagined that my Charles was fond of seeing his children neat and handsome about him."

"You may be as neat as you please," interrupted I, "and I shall love you the better for it; but all this is not neatness, but frippery. These rufflings, and pinkings, and patchings will only make us hated by all the wives of our neighbors. No, my children," continued I, more gravely, "those gowns may be altered into something of a plainer cut; for finery is very unbecoming in us, who want the means of decency. I do not know whether such flouncing and shredding is becoming even in the rich, if we consider that the nakedness of the indigent world may be clothed from the trimmings of the vain."

The remonstrance had the proper effect; they went with great composure, that very instant, to change their dress. The next day I had the satisfaction of finding my daughters, at their own request, employed in cutting up their trains into Sunday waistcoats for Dick and Bill, the two little ones; and what was still more satisfactory, the gowns seemed improved by this curtailing.

Toward the end of the week we received a card from [certain] town ladies in which, with their compliments, they hoped to see all our family at church the Sunday following. All Saturday morning I could perceive in consequence of this, my wife and daughters in close conference together, and now and then glancing at me with looks that betrayed a latent plot.

To be sincere, I had strong suspicious that some absurd proposal was preparing for appearing with splendor the next day. In the evening they began their operations in a very regular manner, and my wife undertook to conduct the siege. After tea, when I seemed in spirits, she began thus: "I fancy, Charles, my dear, we shall have a great deal of good company at our church tomorrow."

"Perhaps we may, my dear," returned I, "though you need be under no uneasiness about that, you shall have a sermon whether there be or not."

"That is what I expect," returned she, "but I think, my dear, we ought to appear there as decently as possible, for who knows what may happen?"

"Your precautions," replied I, "are highly commendable. A decent behavior and appearance in church is what charms me. We should be devout and humble, cheerful and serene."

"Yes," cried she, "I know that, but I mean we should go there in as proper a manner as possible; not altogether like the scrubs about us."

"You are quite right, my dear," returned I, "and I was going to make the very same proposal. The proper manner of going is, to go there as early as possible to have time for meditation before the service begins."

"Phoo, Charles," interrupted she, "all that is very true, but not what I would be at. I mean we should go there genteelly. You know the church is two miles off, and I protest I don't like to see my daughters trudging up to their pew all blowzed and red with walking, and looking for all the world as if they had been winners at a smock race.

"Now, my dear, my proposal is this: there are our two plow horses, the Colt that has been in our family these nine years, and his companion Blackberry, that has scarce done an earthly thing for this month past. They are both grown fat and lazy. Why should not they do something as well as we? And let me tell you, when Moses has trimmed them a little, they will cut a very tolerable figure."

To this proposal I objected that walking would be twenty times more genteel than such a paltry conveyance, as Blackberry was wall-eyed and the Colt wanted a tail; that they had never been broke to the rein; but had a hundred vicious tricks; and that we had but one saddle and pillion in the whole house. All these objections, however, were overruled, and I was obliged to comply.

The next morning I perceived them not a little busy in collecting such materials as might be necessary for the expedition. As I found it would be a business of time, I walked on to the church before, and they promised speedily to follow. I waited near an hour in the reading desk for their arrival; but not finding them come as expected, I was obliged to begin, and went through the service not without some uneasiness at finding them absent.

This was increased when all was finished, and no appearance of the family. I therefore walked back by the horseway, which was five miles round, though the footway was but two. When got about halfway home I perceived the procession marching slowly forward toward the church, my son, my wife, and the two little ones exalted on one horse and my two daughters upon the other.

I demanded the cause of their delay, but soon found by their looks they had met with a thousand misfortunes on the road. The horses at first refused to move from the door, till Mr. Burchell [a friend] was kind enough to beat them forward for about two hundred yards with his cudgel. Next, the straps of my wife's pillion broke down, and they were obliged to stop to repair them before they could proceed.

After that, one of the horses took it to his head to stand still, and neither blows nor entreaties could prevail with him to proceed. He was just recovering from this dismal situation when I found them; but perceiving everything safe, I own their present mortification did not displease me, as it would give me many opportunities of future triumph, and teach my daughters more humility.

---

[1]Goldsmith's novel, *The Vicar of Wakefield,* from which these passages are taken, was first published in London in 1766, and has appeared since in hundreds of editions. The excerpts are from chapters 1, 4 and 10 of an edition published by Huron Books, London, n.d.

Classic 19th Century Christian Humor

Waiting and Hoping

by Samuel Porter Jones

Preaching the Gospel was not something Sam Jones (1847-1906) took lightly. For him it was a life-and-death matter. He was one of the greatest soul-winners of his generation, and his message changed the face of many an American city. At the same time he could not help being Sam Jones, which meant that his preaching was highly entertaining. People who cared little for his Gospel were fascinated by the way he presented it. Born and reared in rural Georgia, delivered from alcoholism at his father's deathbed, converted to Christ, he became one of America's most colorful evangelists. Let's join the packed audience gathered in the year 1885 in Sam's Gospel tent in Nashville, Tennessee, while he is speaking:[1]

—

These revival services are to get men willing to be saved, not to get God willing to save them. You understand that: it is God's accepted time. You will never see the gates wider open than they are now. You may get in after awhile, but if you don't go in now the chances are against you. In Hell you will carry the recollection that you stood once in this city right before the open gates of God's mercy and grace and would not enter.

There are plenty of people that want to go to Heaven on their own schedule. They want to drink a little, lie a little, and gamble occasionally. This suggests the story of the lady whose daughter's tooth ached. She sent for a dentist. He came and pulled out a pair of big, old-fashioned forceps. The lady screamed, "Don't put them things in my daughter's mouth. Pull it with your fingers!"

That would be mighty nice if it could be done. God bless you all. If you will let me get the old Gospel forceps and take hold of those teeth, I will bring them out; but I can't pull them with my fingers.

Do you know the terms on which God will take hold of you and carry you through this world and safely up to Heaven? You just lay down those things that are hurting you, and take up those other things that will help you, and you will have His help in time and eternity. Why will a man ask better terms than that he quit those things that damage him on earth and in Heaven?

One sinner says, "I know that right is right and wrong is wrong. I am waiting for the church to get right." You will be in Hell a million years before that happens. A man is in mighty poor business haggling around at these members of the church. Many of them are on the road tonight, coming back. They did not know how low down they were.

"I am waiting for feeling," says some fellow. You look at me. You are an honest, sensible citizen of this town. What do you mean by feelings? Once I went down into the congregation and said to an old sinner, "Come up and give your heart to God." He said, "Mr. Jones, I have not got a bit of feeling." And he could hardly stand on his feet, he had so much. When a man sees he ought to do right and quit the wrong, that's the only feeling there is on the subject. Do you think that you ought to be a Christian, and ought to start tonight? If you do, you have got feeling enough to sweep you right under the cross.

Another fellow says, "I am not waiting for feeling, I am waiting until I am fit." Yes, you take the most intelligent lawyer out of Christ in this town, and the most ignorant man, and say to the ignorant one, "Tom, do you belong to the church?"

"No, sir, 'cause I ain't fitten."

Then you meet the lawyer and ask the same question and he will reply, "Why I am not fit, sir, to be a member of the church."

Is it not astonishing that they meet on precisely the same road? "I am waiting until I am fit." When you analyze that thing in the light of the Gospel, it is the most ridiculous position a man can put himself in. Here is a fellow starving to death; there is a richly-loaded table.

"Are you hungry?"

"Yes, as hungry as I can be, but I can't go to that table, my hands ain't fitten."

"Here are soap and water and towels."

He says, "I ain't fitten to wash."

You come up and join the church. Don't hang back and say, "I am not fitten." Come up here and get "fitten." But he will say, "I ain't fitten to get fitten." What are you going to do with that sort of man? Let me tell you that the very fact that you don't feel fit is the thing that commends you to God. I have never felt worthy of membership in the church of Jesus Christ. If you wait until you are worthy to join the church, you will wait until millions of years shall have rolled away.

I like to see a man just walk up and get his ticket, jump on the train and move off. The difficulty with some of us is, we buy our tickets to way-stations and never get through. Let us get a limited ticket clear through to the next world, and into Heaven we will ride. Don't trouble yourself about the destination; stick to the train and you will land in Heaven.

Don't act like that fellow who said, "I want to go to Chattanooga, but I am afraid I can't get through."

"This is the train," said the conductor. "We are going that way now."

As the train pulled out of the station the fellow said, "I wouldn't miss it for all the world."

"Keep your seat," said the conductor, "and we'll take you to Chattanooga."

When they reached Stevenson he said, "I am so afraid we won't get to Chattanooga."

"Keep your seat," said the conductor, "and we'll take you to Chattanooga."

At Bridgeport the man said, "I am troubled a good deal about getting to Chattanooga."

"Keep your seat."

As the whistle blew for Chattanooga he said, "I am afraid I will miss it."

"Keep your seat."

As the train rolled into the car shed at Chattanooga he was still giving vent to his fear about missing the place.

An old church member said to me, "I have so many dark days. I do want to get to Heaven." Keep your seat! The train goes through. We will get there, thank God! Sister, keep your seat, it will go through. Brother, keep your head in at the window, the train is in good hands.

Another says, "I am waiting for faith." Yes, you have been waiting forty years for faith. How much have you saved up? Like the fellow who had ten bushels of wheat, and was waiting till more grew before he would sow what he had. Sow it, and you will have a hundredfold. By keeping it you will not get any more, but the rats will eat up what you have.

There is not a man in this tent who has not got enough faith ultimately to save his soul if he will use what he has. You use what you have and you will get more. What tickles me is to hear a fellow down praying for faith. "Lord, give me faith." That ain't Scriptural. Christ rebuked those who prayed for faith. You use the faith you have. I would as soon pray for sweet potatoes as for faith.

My hope is in God. My hope is not in riches, or in my friends, or my pastor, or the church, or my father and mother, or my wife, with all her fondness and love for me. My hope is in God.

Let us make a start. The question is not, "Have I got enough religion to take me to Heaven?" The question is whether I have enough to start. Enough to say, "Right is right and I am going to do it. Wrong is wrong, and I am going to quit it."

When traveling by train in Georgia I frequently ride on the engine. One time while I stood in the cab, admiring the locomotive that was to draw our train from Atlanta to Chattanooga, I heard the engineer ask his fireman, "Have we enough steam to start with?"

The reply was, "Yes, sir."

On looking at the steam gauge, I observed that the register was about sixty pounds, and the capacity of the boiler was one hundred and forty pounds. I wondered why so light a pressure was deemed sufficient; but the train had not reached the Chattahoochee river, less than seven miles away, before I saw the engine blowing off steam; it already had too much. The engine generated steam faster when running than when stationary.

Glory to God! We generate power while in motion faster than when standing still. Lord Jesus Christ, let men see that all they need to do is to step out in the right direction! Where the road is rough the repair shops are thick, and as sure as you live, they hold out to the next world.

The fact is, a man gets religion a good deal like he gets the measles. It's catching. A fellow goes and gets tangled up with the measles, and in about ten days he says, "Wife, you can send for the doctor. I feel bad; I ache from head to foot." She sends for a doctor, and he comes and examines the case.

He asks, "Have you been exposed to measles? That is what you have got." He gives him a cup of good hot tea, and says, "You keep on drinking that until you get it broke out on you, and then you will be all right."

Now, some of you have got tangled up in this meeting, and you never felt so mean in your life. You have caught religion. I will just give you two or three cups of Gospel tea, and break it out on you; then keep it broke out, and you are elected. Take two or three cups of this warm tea, and then you will be saved. Break it out and keep it broke out. Religion is like measles; if it goes in on you it will kill you. The trouble with a great many Christians in this city is, religion has gone in on them. Wrap up and keep warm, and keep it broke out on hands, feet and tongue.

What is repentance? It is quitting my devilment. If my boy does any devilment, the best repentance he can do is quit. What sort of repentance do I want? I want quitting repentance. That is what we call evangelical repentance—the sort these sinners want. They don't want legal repentance. They are like the Irishman who said about justice, "Faith, that is just what I *don't* want!" Evangelical repentance is quitting. I won't do it any more.

Repentance is the first conscious movement of the soul from sin toward God. Many a fellow is praying for rain with his tub the wrong side up. God cannot fill a tub when it is wrong side up without inverting the law of gravity. God is holding up His clouds for you while you are holding your tub the wrong side up.

It is not asking much of you to ask you to believe on the Lord Jesus Christ. I believed on Him for twenty-five years, but I did not believe on Him as much as the Devil did. He believed and trembled; I believed and went on drinking. Now I believe on the Lord Jesus Christ in the sense that I will follow Him. I am not running on understanding. I could not get to my front gate on understanding. I love Him.

The train is here; the bell is ringing to start; I step aboard, and move out tonight for the good world. Will you go? There are five hundred persons here this evening whom I want to see on these front pews. Some of you are already on them. It is a quarter past eight o'clock. We have plenty of time. I want to see every man who has no religion here tonight. I want to take your hand and help you to start to Heaven.

Will you believe tonight? Will you confess tonight? Will you say, "I consecrate my life to Christ. I make Him my Savior, and will do His will from this time on and forever"? I want every man in this tent tonight who feels as if he wants to take the essential step that will bring him to God, to rise up, and we will pray for him.

---

[1]Some faithful transcriber took down this message in shorthand as Sam Jones delivered it in a gospel tent in Nashville, Tennessee, in May, 1885. It was edited that same year by W. M. Leftwich, and published in 1885 by the Southern Methodist Publishing House as *Sermons and Sayings* by the Rev. Sam P. Jones.

Classic 20th Century Christian Humor

DON'T HELP THAT BEAR!

by Sandy Dengler[1]

Sandy Dengler is an outdoorswoman. She is also a talented author of Christian fiction, and has pursued a unique career as naturalist, medical technician, livestock wrangler, teacher, and (for over thirty years) the wife of Bill Dengler, National Park ranger. Her experiences have ranged from milking the poison from scorpions, to hiking barefoot to the bottom of the Grand Canyon. Equipped with two university degrees, Sandy became a prolific writer following her conversion to Christ during a 1969 Billy Graham television crusade. Her published books, which number well over fifty, include Christian biographies, historical fiction and juvenile mysteries. The Denglers have two grown daughters and currently make their home in Ashford, Washington, on the edge of Mount Rainier

National Park. Sandy combines her joy-filled Christian witness with a droll wit, and she is always an entertaining speaker. Her bear story is a worthy example of humorous Christian writing of the 20th century.

To us who are part of the ranger-naturalist family, Yosemite National Park in California is famous for more than its majestic scenery. Let others toast the stupendous wonders, the continent's greatest monolith, El Capitan, the magnificent Half Dome, and the world class waterfalls. We in the family, who know the Park intimately, like to think of it as the renowned home of nature's brainiest, connivingest, and most perspicacious quadrupeds, the Yosemite black bears.

Posted rules abound in National Parks to protect campers against marauding bears, and they may work dandy elsewhere, but not in Yosemite. "Keep coolers and food in the car trunk. Hang anything that smells like food (such as apple-scented shampoo) from the steel cables provided at campsite. Place all garbage in bearproof dumpsters. Never approach a bear with food in your hand, and never defend your grub."

The trouble is that bears never read the rules. One mama bear sent her cub up a tree and out on a limb to the cable where it chewed through the knot, thus depositing an entire camper's food cache at mama's feet. Another boosted her cub into the bearproof dumpster. Still another bear devised a method to get into a car trunk. Simply hook your claws onto the top of the closed window, smash the window with one yank, and rip out the back seat. Chow down! If the vehicle is a convertible, no problem. Tear off the top and it's a smorgasbord.

My personal introduction to the Yosemite bear came one fine summer day when I decided it was time to learn to fish. My ranger husband, Bill, had regaled me with the delights of catching a Golden Trout, unique to the western slope of the Sierra Nevada. I read some books on the subject, and decided it was a piece of cake. You take along a selection of baits, match the fish's appetite to the preferred morsel, cast and haul in.

So, equipped with a light windbreaker, I set out, following a trail that led upstream beside the south fork of the Merced river. The trail soon became faint, but I espied a deep pool below a stretch of riffles. What a lovely eden it proved to be. Red fir and ponderosa pines... Chickadees discussing whether to nest there or migrate upstream, where they would hang upside down from the pine cones... Skies above the valley a luscious blue... The touch of a zephyr on my cheek... Joy... Peace... God.

But the fish would not bite. Hours passed, and soon the sun sank behind the crags. I tried lure after lure without success. Then after a long day my bobber finally bobbed. A nibble! But it was growing time to start back, or I would have trouble in the gloom finding that faint trail. Yet the thrill of catching something was so close! Discarding all my nifty lures and bait, I reeled in and put a plain, fresh worm on the hook.

It worked. There was the barest suggestion of a tug on the line. Gently, smoothly, I set the hook. The sweet joy of success came as I realized I was outwitting a creature with a brain that could fit into an eyedropper with plenty of room for drops. It was a good-sized trout, five or six inches, maybe seven. I was groping on the streambank for my borrowed net when behind me I heard a distinctive sound, very close.

"Woof!"

I turned and looked. The bear was the color they call cinnamon, a dirty reddish, rather dark in the waning light. It stood squarely on the trail facing me. The fish, having come to the surface, was tugging and flopping in a way the bear apparently found most enticing. All escape for me was cut off. A thick growth of saplings and riparian brush surrounded the stream edge.

It sounds crazy, but all I could think of at the moment was a childhood ditty about an old southern preacher who went hunting and ran into a grizzly bear. The words of his prayer came to me:

> "O Lord, didn't You deliver Daniel from the lions' den,
> Also delivered Jonah from the belly of the whale, and then,
> Three Hebrew children from the fiery furnace, so the Good Book doth declare;
> Now Lord, if You can't help me, for goodness' sake don't You help that bear!"

Bears outweigh human beings four or five to one. On the other hand, most bears' brains are much smaller than humans'. Some guides recommend opening the zipper of one's windbreaker with both hands, spreading the jacket wide and presenting a formidable, massive appearance. I didn't try that. Instead I dropped the fishpole and negotiated the swift current of the Merced somewhat faster than the speed of light. It is clear however I did not walk on the water, for I found myself wet and dripping on the opposite bank.

Looking back across, I saw that the bear had skidded down the bank, snatched up my fish, clambered back and was now disappearing into the brush, carrying in his jaws the fruit of my day's work.

When I returned to camp, still shaking, and told my harrowing story to Bill and our friends, their reaction was most unsatisfactory. Instead of thanking God for my narrow escape, they considered the whole episode hilarious, and joined in siding with that stupid, thieving bear. After all my striving, here was my first fish, stolen, and there they were, sending up a merry cheer for the creature who did nothing to earn his tasty morsel.

That's life in the Park family, and you can see that we face a conundrum of nature. Do we protect the fish from the fisherman? The fisherman from the bear? The bear from the tourist? Do we turn nature loose and watch what happens, or do we nudge her gently in a preferred direction? If the latter, where do visitors with shredded car tops enter into the equation? Our National Parks need public support to survive, but the public will not long support something they cannot learn to appreciate, or with which they cannot fall in love.

The National Park does not belong to the fisherman, or the fish, or the bears, or even the government. The Park belongs to God who made it. For thousands of years the land that now forms our National Parks was here before we decided to protect it from ourselves. We have learned that in today's pollution-ridden environment we desperately need the parks more than ever for the health of our souls. But more than the parks, we need God.

Here is a curious analogy. Much of the Bible has been around for thousands of years, but today a strong move is afoot to clean up God's Word by keeping whatever a panel of experts decides is "authentic" and dropping the rest. In the same way a move has been afoot to rid Yosemite Park of some of its bears. The troublemakers would be shipped to other parts—Idaho, perhaps. That would permit convertibles to navigate the streets of the valley without having their tops ripped off. And maybe then I could keep my fish.

But there are those of us who love the Bible and know it to be a wild and exuberant piece, with dark corners and glorious mountain tops and superb challenges and deep actions of God that are beyond understanding. We don't want our wild Bible tamed by academicians (who probably never visited a National Park.). God's Word is awesome. It has stood solid for all these millenia, and has become a light to the human race of truth and goodness. It has borne a Heaven-sent message of faith and love and salvation. Leave it in its wild and joyous state.

In the same way I'm glad to know they have decided to suffer the bears to stay in Yosemite. Leave them alone! "Don't help that bear!" If the naughty ones had gone, they would have taken with them part of the exciting fun and joy and wild exuberance of life on this planet. Visitors to a tamed Park would have been more comfortable in territory free from unexpected challenges, such as the need to think fast and pray, "Lord, don't help that bear!" But Yosemite, our matchless, awe-inspiring piece of earth, would no longer have been whole.

As I reflect on this story, it's evident that God did help my perspicacious bear just as much as He did me. Show me any other bear that can get a human to fish for him!

---

[1]"Don't Help That Bear!" © 1994 by Sandy Dengler, is an original story and is used by permission of the author. All rights reserved. Correspondence should be addressed to Mrs. Dengler at 112 Tahoma Woods, Ashford, WA 98304.

Stories Heard At the Church Coffee Urn

Some readers might like to know where the author picked up these gems of whimsy. He is happy to respond in the words that the poet Henry Wadsworth Longfellow wrote at the opening of his *Song of Hiawatha.*

> Should you ask me whence these stories?
> I should answer, I should tell you,
> From the land of the Ojibways,
> In the moorlands and the fen-lands,
> Chetowaik, the plover, sang them,
> Mahng, the loon, the wild-goose, Wawa,
> The blue heron, the Shuh-shuh-gah,
> And the grouse, the Mushkodasa!

Bow Tie

The great Baptist preacher C. Oscar Johnson was in a hotel room dressing himself for a banquet. A man knocked at his door and was invited in. "Sir," he said, "I'm here to escort you to the banquet."

Dr. Johnson said, "Can you help me with this black bow

tie? It won't stay straight."

"Certainly," said the man. He put his hand on Dr. Johnson's back and laid him on the bed, after which he tied the bow knot quickly and neatly.

Dr. Johnson stood up, glanced in the mirror and said, "Good. But why did you make me lie down?"

"It's the only way I can do it," said the man. "I'm an undertaker."

Fooled

A little boy ran to his mother and said, "There's a lion in our backyard!" She looked out the window and saw a large Newfoundland dog had been trimmed like a lion.

"Sonny," she told her boy, "You knew that was just a big dog. Now you go upstairs and tell God about it and ask Him to forgive you for lying."

In a few moments the boy came downstairs and his mother said, "Did you ask forgiveness?"

"Yes, I did," he replied, "and do you know what God said to me? He said, 'That big dog had me fooled too!' "

Perfect

The pastor of a small rural church opened his sermon on Sunday morning with an impressive statement. "Apart from the Son of God," he said, "there has never been a perfect man."

A stranger who had slipped into a rear pew unexpectedly rose to his feet. "Reverend," he said, "I apologize for the interruption, but I must contradict you. I have certainly heard of a perfect man."

Surprised, the minister asked, "Sir, who is he?"
"He was my wife's first husband."

Briefing

The pupils at Cheam School, one of the most respected boys' schools in England, were being briefed for the expected visit next day of Lord Geoffrey Fisher, the Archbishop of Canterbury. They were told, "If the archbishop speaks to you, you must address him as either 'My lord' or 'Your grace.' "

When the distinguished cleric arrived complete with gaiters, the boys were marshaled in a row, shoes shined and cheeks scrubbed. The archbishop walked along the line smiling and stopped to speak to one boy.

"How old are you, sonny?" he asked.

The boy spoke up: "My God, I'm ten!"

Warning

A young preacher had taken as his text one Sunday a verse from the Book of Revelation: "Behold, I come quickly." He became stuck on that particular verse and out of nervousness kept leaning on the rather flimsy pulpit while he repeated, "Behold, I come quickly."

Eventually the preacher lost his balance and fell into the lap of a lady who was sitting in the front pew. Scrambling to his feet, he begged the lady's forgiveness: "Please, ma'am, forgive me. I'm so sorry."

To which the lady replied, "That's all right, young man. You gave me plenty of warning that you were coming. I just didn't have sense enough to get out of the way."

Flood

A Christian brother, when he was a small boy, had been caught in the disastrous Johnstown, Pennsylvania, flood of 1889. The Conemaugh River dam above the city burst after heavy rains and 2,200 persons were drowned. After he grew up it became an obsession with this man to talk about the "Johnstown flood."

In due course he died and went to Heaven, where Peter asked him what he would like to do. He said, "I'd like to get some people together and tell them about the Johnstown flood." The apostle said he thought that could be arranged. Within a short time the man was informed that a group had come together and he was welcome to talk to them about the Johnstown flood.

As the man was about to step to the podium to commence his address, Peter spoke to him privately. "I think you ought to know," he said, "that Noah is in the audience."

Dog Out

A young preacher had been called to a small rural church and appeared for his first sermon on Sunday morning. To his dismay he found that one of the parishioners had brought his dog to the service. During the opening hymn he spoke politely to the dog's owner and asked if he would kindly remove the animal. The man obligingly took the dog out, then returned to his seat.

After the service the deacons of the church waited on the new preacher and rebuked him for insulting one of their staunch members. They pointed out that the dog made no trouble; he had been accompanying his master to church for years. The young man was abashed at what he had done. That afternoon he called at the home of the dog's owner and made his apology. He said he had no intention of creating a problem in the church on his first Sunday, and was very sorry indeed.

The man was quite friendly. He said, "Don't worry a bit about it, Reverend. It all worked out. I wouldn't have had my dog hear that sermon for anything in the world."

Kiss

The Irish girl confessed to her priest that she allowed her sweetheart to kiss her. The priest asked, "How long ago did this happen?"

She said, "Ten years ago, and I've confessed it several times."

He said, "You don't have to confess it but once."

"I know," she replied, "but it's a pleasant memory and I like to talk about it."

Difference

A father was reading when his young son came to him and said, "Dad, our teacher said today that we came from monkeys. Did we?"

The father replied, "Perhaps you did. I didn't."

The boy went on, "It makes no difference to me whether or not my grandfather was an ape."

"Maybe it doesn't," said his father, "but it would have made a lot of difference to your grandmother."

Flowers

After attending a church couples' retreat, a man decided to do something about his domestic difficulties. The following Monday he stopped in at a florist's on the way home from work and bought a dozen red and pink carnations. Instead of walking in the front door, he rang the bell. His wife opened the door, looked at the flowers and burst into tears.

"Darling, what's the matter?" he asked.

"Oh, Jim," she wept, "It has been a dreadful day. The children have been fighting, the sink is stopped up, the washing machine sprang a leak, the dog got into the garbage, and now you come home drunk!"

Cut

A minister appeared in the pulpit one Sunday morning with a small band-aid on his cheek. At the close of the service as he was standing by the door, a little elderly lady asked him, "How did you hurt yourself?"

"Why, I was concentrating on my sermon while I was shaving," he explained, "and I cut myself."

"That's too bad," she said soothingly. "Why didn't you concentrate on your shaving and cut your sermon?"

Flag

Most church sanctuaries position flags on either side of the chancel, the American flag on the right, another flag on the left. A small boy and his mother were sitting in a pew as the Sunday morning service was about to begin. He pointed to the other flag and whispered, "What's that flag for?"

She explained, "That's for the people who died in the Service."

He thought about it a moment and asked, "Nine-thirty or eleven o'clock?"

Kind Word

A minister entered a small restaurant in a strange town and found it had only one waitress. When she came to take his order she seemed in a rather dour mood.

"What'll you have?" she asked.

He smiled at her. "A boiled egg and a kind word."

She brought his order and placed it in front of him. He looked up .

"Where's the kind word?" he asked.

She said, "Don't eat the egg."

Not Here

An American Baptist lady entered an English cathedral to attend the morning service. She listened with great interest as the reader at the lectern gave out the morning lesson. He read, "And as in Adam all die, even so in Christ shall all be made alive."

"Praise the Lord," she exclaimed. There was a slight stir in the congregation.

The man continued to read: "But now is Christ risen from the dead and become the first fruits of them that slept."

"Hallalujah," she shouted.

A steward tiptoed to her aisle. "Madam," he said, "This

is God's house. We must ask you to be quiet and reverent during the service of worship."

She smiled. "But I've got religion!" she exclaimed.

"Well," he pointed out, "you didn't get it in here."

Bologna

A minister was telling a children's story during the morning service. He said, "It was a cold morning, boys and girls, and a little sparrow sat on a fence shivering and hungry. A butcher's delivery boy happened to drive by and threw a piece of bologna toward it. The sparrow fluttered down, picked it up and flew back on the fencepost, where it began to chirp its thanksgiving for a good meal.

"Just then a hawk heard the sparrow, swooped down and carried it away. Now what does that tell you, children?"

A boy spoke up: "It tells me that when you are full of bologna you'd better keep your mouth shut."

Time

A man arriving at the gate of Heaven met the apostle Peter and asked him, "How do you reckon time up here?"

Peter answered, "A million years is the same as a minute, and a minute the same as a million years."

"Then," said the brother, "how do you value money?"

Peter said, "A million dollars is the same as a penny, and a penny the same as a million dollars."

"Then," said the man, "will you give me a penny?"

Peter replied, "In a minute."

Gavel

A long-winded chairman was conducting a church annual meeting that lasted until late. Finally one of the elders sitting in the front row fell asleep and began to snore. This made the chairman so indignant that he threw his gavel at the elder and struck him on the head. As the man sank into unconsciousness he was heard to murmur, "Hit me again, I can still hear him!"

Charity

Three nuns were left one hundred dollars apiece by a deceased friend. Two decided to donate their money to a favorite charity. The third said she would give hers to a poor, shabbily-dressed man she had seen standing on the corner by a store. She thought he seemed depressed.

The next time she passed the store she slipped a hundred dollars into the man's pocket and whispered, "Never despair!"

Two days later the same man saw her passing, walked up and placed several hundred dollars in her hand. "You were lucky," he said, "Never Despair won the fifth race yesterday and paid seven to one."

Bale of Hay

At a church convention the delegates argued for two hours with increasing irritation about adopting a unified budget for the missionary program. Finally Dr. James Whitcomb Brougher rose to his feet.

"This debate," he said, "reminds me of a jury in Los

Angeles. After arguing about a case a long time, the foreman asked the judge for further instructions. The judge told the jury, 'Go back and if you have not reached a verdict by dinnertime, I will send in twelve dinners and let you continue by holding a night session.'

"At first the foreman agreed. Then he added, 'Your honor, when you send in those dinners, make it eleven dinners and one bale of hay.'"

At the church convention, the laughter was subsiding after Dr. Brougher finished his story when one high-pitched voice called out, "What did they want the bale of hay for?"

Uproar followed. The vote was quickly taken and the decision was unanimous. Nobody wanted to receive the bale of hay.

Dangling

Several years ago newspapers carried the story of a United States Air Force sergeant who recited the 145th Psalm while dangling by his left foot from an unopened parachute. He was one of six crewmen aboard a C-47 prop transport when the pilot lost control of his equipment in a swirling snowstorm over Nebraska.

The sergeant had been reading Psalm 145 during the flight. As he faced his first jump, he failed to fasten his harness securely. While upside down in a free fall through the icy air, he managed to double his body and catch the harness above his foot. During this time he was saying the words of the Psalm:

> The Lord upholds all those who fall and lifts up all who are bowed down.

After climbing to a sitting position, the sergeant reached for the ripcord and landed safely.

Any Minute Now

The congregation of the First Methodist Church of Houston, Texas, presented its distinguished pastor, Dr. Charles Allen, with a new color television set on an anniversary Sunday. That afternoon, his morning services over, Dr. Allen settled in his easy chair to watch the Raiders play the Cowboys. Mrs. Allen spoke gently to her husband, suggesting that perhaps the congregation did not present them with the new set for watching football on the Lord's Day.

"Don't think a thing about it, Mother," said Dr. Allen. "Just leave it where it is; Billy Graham will be coming on any minute now."

Some Well-Seasoned Advice to Young Men from an Old Hand:

Strive toward a noble goal in life. As the girl said to her boy friend when he kissed her chin, "Aim higher, young man!"

—

Jesus took a strong stand against polygamy. He said, "No man can serve two masters" (Luke 16:13).

—

One zealous young man wrote to his girl faithfully every day for six months. She married the postman.

PART FIVE

Rx: Happy Ending

Perhaps by now, in the grace of God, you have arrived in Joy Country. If not, you might be on your way. Hallelujah! If the stories told at the church coffee urn did not entertain you, ignore them and press on. The whole intent of these pages is not to evoke a laugh, but to help you understand that God wants you to enjoy yourself. He has a much better set of pleasures than the Epicureans and hedonists, and more attractive personnel.

Now for a good story to wind up things. It will end (almost) in a kiss, in the delightful way that English novels used to end. But it will also indulge a look back, which sometimes makes the present easier to take.

Write me, if you are in a jovial mood. I'd like to hear from you.

S.E.W.

A Tar and His Feathers

Before we embark on the romantic journey that closes this book of joy, I would like to insert a scholarly note. Many distinguished authorities on the subject of joy have stated in one way or another that *real joy is rooted in sorrow and woe.* Thus Alexander Maclaren, a noted Scottish divine, declared, "The highest joy to the Christian almost always comes through suffering." Even the great Charles Spurgeon said, "There is a sweet joy that comes to us through sorrow." And a religious editor told a writer friend of mine that "Christians don't buy humor books unless there's a tragedy involved!"

Now, I have a rather oafish mind, but as a Christian I have been through my portion of grief and never thought it was either funny or joyful. Nevertheless I am pleased to know about the close link between sorrow and joy, because it gives me an excuse to describe in the context of joy the sorriest trip I ever took in my life.

—

My tale of the Threadbare Thirties is about a leaky, rusty old scow that stank of raw sugar from stem to stern and boom to bilge; and about the most maladapted, unlikely landlubber that ever shipped out under the colors of the United States Merchant Marine.

It's inconceivable how I got shanghaied aboard such a derelict when I thought I was signing on to be a cadet on a luxury cruise liner bound from San Francisco to Sydney, Australia. But let's not bother with that dismal turn of events. The real woe starts when this goldbricking homeboy, this English major who didn't know a scupper from a capstan and didn't care, was hired aboard the S.S. *Maunalei* of the Matson Navigation Company.

I must elucidate a few things about our Love Boat. It was not small, for it had five booms with hatches. Its commission was to convey raw sugar from the plantations of Hawaii to the huge refinery at Crockett on upper San Francisco Bay. It had a midship house, steam turbines, twin screws, and it burned oil. For the crew it provided a most uncomfortable fo'c'sle in the wrong place, under the sternwheel, where the groans of the rudder machinery periodically intruded on the sleep of the swabs.

A word should also be said about our chain of command. On the bridge (where I was never allowed) was the ship's captain who, as far as I was aware, never spoke to anyone. Next was Mr. John Blain, the first mate, who spoke to everyone in a threatening foghorn voice and made effective use of a seasoned vocabulary. The second and third mates hardly mattered, and the engineers spent most of their time under blowers below decks.

The next man of parts was the bosun, a short Portuguese-Hawaiian citizen with the Irish name of Murphy and a surly disposition. He bossed a crew of several Hawaiian sailors, plus one Swede who told us he came from Lapland (but as it turned out, he was from Shakopee, Minnesota). These men were A.B.'s, or able-bodied seamen. I also held an A.B. of sorts from the University of California, but it did not signify on this vessel. One or two crewmen who had not attained A.B. status were called O.S.'s, or ordinary seamen.

You have now reached the bottom of the list, except for one. I was also a member of Mr. Murphy's crew. I was the deckboy. With the exception of the cockroaches, who were not on payroll, a deckboy was the lowest thing that crawled on the deck of the *Maunalei,* and my fellow crew members wasted no time letting me know it.

We made a three-day voyage up the west coast from San Francisco to Seattle and Tacoma, at which ports we took on cargoes of lumber. We were now cruising through the Straits of Juan de Fuca on our way to Honolulu. The bosun had routed me out early to clean the scuppers and empty the garbage over the side. The seagulls loved my offerings, but I quickly learned which was the windward side of the ship!

The poet Masefield wrote about the "grey mist on the sea's face and the grey dawn breaking,"[1] and on this particular morning he was half right. A grey dawn was breaking and a grey mist surrounded the old tub, but it wasn't "on the sea's face," it was in my face. Off the port side were the uninviting rocks of Cape Flattery, the last land we would see for nine days. *Aieuw!*

The chores finished, I stopped by a companionway to drink at the little fountain. One mouthful and I gagged and spat. Salt!

"What's happened?" I demanded of Upili, a crew member.

He grinned wickedly. "Pilikea," he said. "Leak. Double bottom." So we would be using salt water for the next nine days. By this time the ship was pitching and yawing, and my stomach felt as if beetles were moving around inside it.

Joseph Conrad once wrote a eulogy about a ship on which he sailed as a young man. "Oh, youth!" he exclaimed. "The strength of it, the imagination of it! To me she was not an old rattletrap carting about the world a lot of coal for a freight—to me she was the endeavor, the test, the trial of life."

I will not comment beyond saying that I was not a Christian at the time and had no desire to take on any more endeavors, tests, or trials. But ah, wait.

I was emerging from the midship house onto the main deck when a new and different smell assailed my nostrils. In Tacoma we had apparently taken aboard a cargo not just of lumber, but of chickens! I located them just aft the cook's galley, forty-four crates of them including a dozen roosters, all squawking their heads off.

As I leaned over to inspect them the first mate, Mr. Blain, came alongside and stood with fists on hips. "From now to Honolulu," he snapped at me, "you will take care of these birds. Feed and water twice a day, and no dead ones. Understand?" As he turned around I felt a nip on the back of my hand. An ugly Rhode Island Red rooster was giving me a vicious look. It was to be war to the finish.

Half a dozen hens were in each crate, and outside the chicken wire of the crates were two coffee cans to be filled with water, with a trough between them for grain feed. So far, so good, but now I was to learn what the psychologists like to speak of as the "pecking order." They learned it from the chickens.

Within two days I discovered that in each crate, one chicken becomes the boss. She can peck every other hen, and none of the others can peck her. Next is the Number Two hen, which can peck every other hen except the queen who rules the roost, and who pecks her. Then the Number Three hen pecks three others, and gets pecked in turn by the two at the top. The sad sack at the bottom is the hen who gets pecked by all the other five.

In a very short time this hen was reduced to a pitiable condition. Its rear end was ripped loose and hung down, dripping blood. To save its life I had to remove it from the coop, but where to put it? If I transferred it to another crate it would be attacked *en masse* because of the blood. There were no spare crates. If I let it die I would be held accountable. There was nothing to do but turn it loose on the deck. In the process I got pecks from all six hens in the crate.

But there were forty-four crates, and the pecking order was in full uproar in all of them. Each day at sea conditions grew worse. The loose chickens began exploring the passageways. One entered the chief engineer's stateroom and promptly threw up, no doubt from drinking salt water. The chief caught it, pitched it over the side, and then pitched into me with several epithets in the language of the day. Other loose hens found life outside the crate lonesome, and sought fellowship with the fowls still in the coops. This they achieved by flopping into the feed troughs and upsetting the water cans. In due time the grain responded to the soaking, nature took its course, and grass began to sprout in mid-Pacific.

My fellow shipmates, the members of the crew, proved to be more than interested observers of my charges. Some of the hens were laying, and I began to notice empty eggshells around the crates. The sailors were sneaking over when I was away, stealing eggs out of the crates, biting holes in the end of each egg, and sucking out the raw whites and yolks.

On the final day out before we reached Honolulu I had

thirty badly-pecked chickens running around on the main deck. There were chickens in the cook's galley, chickens on the hatch covers, chickens in the rag locker, the carpenter shop, the bosun's locker, the engineers' staterooms, the boat deck, the shelter deck, even the wheel house. They couldn't quite reach the bridge or the crow's nest, but everywhere they went they left feathers and messes. Chickens even appeared fricasseed at the officers' mess.

The more I tried to help the miserable creatures, the more I appeared negligent of my duty. Being low on the pecking order myself, my only recourse as I saw it was to keep my mouth shut when the ship's officers were around, and to sass the rest of the crew. I tried putting six of the most mutilated cases in one crate, but when I did, the pecking order was immediately established all over again. I even put six of the worst top peckers in one crate and invited the crew to watch the free-for-all championship match, but it proved to be a standoff.

On the afternoon of that last day at sea I set out to round up the loose flock. This involved the risk of being severely pecked on arms and legs. The method I devised was to grasp a hen by one leg and start swinging it in a 360-degree circle while I pirouetted about the deck. The bird tried valiantly to reach me with its beak, but I swung harder. Eventually it drooped and I tossed it into a crate.

By next morning all the hens were back in their crates except for the few that went to Davy Jones' locker or into the stomachs of the first, second and third mates. I went on deck to be greeted by a glorious sunrise and a gaggle of sailboats, pleasure craft, tug boats and screeching sea fowl. The *Maunalei,* having polluted the Pacific Ocean for nine days, was now rounding Diamond Head and heading into

Honolulu harbor, where it docked at the Aloha Tower. My duties done, I went below to discover that a silver dollar (one day's work) had been lifted from my clothes.[2]

---

[1]From John Masefield, "Sea Fever," in his *Poems,* New York, Macmillan, 1945, p. 10.

[2]The author served on the deck crew aboard the freighter S.S. *Maunalei* of the Matson Navigation Company on a voyage from San Francisco to Hilo, Hawaii, via Seattle, Tacoma, and island sugar ports, September–October, 1933.

A Sentimental Journey

O joy too high for my low style to show!
O bliss fit for a nobler state than me!

—Philip Sidney

"Seventy-five and half alive." Those were my feelings as I entered the new year of 1987. The joy of being filled with the Holy Spirit was still with me, but my wife of forty-six years had left me for Heaven. In the months that had passed since her homegoing, I longed to follow her. A lengthy attack of Taiwan throat had destroyed my appetite and left me with a wheeze. I was about ready to take in the rat guards, coil up the heaving lines, weigh anchor and ship out. Death held no sting for me. God had been good, and life had turned out far better than I had dreamed. I could leave this earth with few regrets and with all my sins forgiven. Jesus and Heaven formed an appealing prospect.

It was in that kind of mood that I picked up the telephone one January day and called the business number of an old friend in Winnipeg, Manitoba, hoping to forget myself in a congenial chat.

It had been years since I had seen Ruth Love. A sympathy card from her had been the only recent contact. We had worked together on the Billy Graham evangelistic team for many years, but had seldom encountered each other. When we did, it was with a brief smile and a handshake.

What could I have been thinking of in placing such a call? In all those years I don't recall ever talking to her on the telephone. What could I say? She was managing a busy office with weighty responsibilities. I was a retired senior citizen, a vulnerable lonely widower who lived in an empty house two thousand miles from Winnipeg.

Ruth was cordial enough after the initial surprise of the call, but it did not take long for her to say, "I think you are running up a phone bill."

"May I call you tonight?"

She gave me her home telephone number, but the evening conversation was equally desultory. We ran down the list of mutual friends and chatted about the weather. I offered to send along a copy of my latest book. She thanked me for the thought. Just what it was I had in mind by making the call, she obviously did not know. Neither did I. But later that night as I got ready for bed, my prayer life began to show faint symptoms of revival.

At 75 years of age one does not jump in and out of love. What may seem normal to some young folks is, to a septuagenarian, plain lunacy. Yet as the days progressed, letters were exchanged and I realized that God had set no age limit on pleasant social intercourse. I asked Ruth for a picture and after an interminable wait, it arrived. Things were looking up.

Letters and telephone calls have their limitations, and there came a time when Ruth expressed bewilderment as to where this renewed friendship was heading. Her life, it seems, was well planned. She had four years to go before reaching full retirement age. She would then resign her position and move to Seattle, where her sister's growing family resided. My late entrance into her ordered life threatened to confuse her thinking, as she wrote me.

On the evening of the day I received her letter, I telephoned Ruth and asked if she would join me in prayer. I, too, was wondering about what lay ahead, and wanted to give the Lord all the time He wanted. After we committed both ourselves and our relationship into God's hands, the pressure seemed to lift and we felt relieved. In her next letter Ruth wrote, "When you called and we had prayer together, that said something very special to me about you."

A growing sensation of joy was beginning to pervade both ends of the line of communication. A close friend with whom I shared something of what was happening said, "She sounds like a godly woman to me." It struck me that "a godly woman" was precisely what I needed. Whether the godly woman needed me remained to be seen. Meanwhile my health seemed to be taking a turn for the better. God was at work.

In my next letter to Ruth I wrote, "I have no intention of pushing our relationship faster than God wants. After all, we're not children. We can remain good friends and enjoy each other's fellowship. There is no need to overstep the proprieties and conventions of Christian friendship . . . " Then I added the words, "unless the Red River of the North should suddenly overflow its banks!"

Another conversation on the telephone seemed to go on and on, until at last Ruth told me we ought to bring it to a close. I had made a note as to how I planned to terminate the conversation. "Say something nice to me," I said, "and I'll hang up.'

There was a pause. She said something nice.

Zarooooom! I was thunderstruck. Was she talking to me? *Me?* I muttered something and hung up. My head was whirling. Suddenly the future was opening to me like a palace garden. No more loneliness. No more anxiety or uncertainty. Somebody cherished me, and it was Ruth! God really did care about me. He had heard my plaintive cry and answered it.

I walked over to the piano which I had not touched for five years and got out the music to Schubert's *Serenade,* which I had been trying to play since 1940. I played it, badly, then got in my car and drove to a florist shop, where I wired a dozen red and white carnations to Winnipeg. After that I headed for the nearby hills and climbed my favorite Twin Peaks, where I offered a prayer of thanksgiving.

Joy! Joy! God had poured it out and my cup was running over.

But the time had come to pass up all other forms of communication and appear on the scene in person. We had discussed the possibility of my paying a visit to Winnipeg for a weekend. We would make it purely a friendly visit, take in the symphony, go for a ride—that sort of thing. I would stay at a hotel.

A month later came the sentimental journey to Manitoba. In an active life I had made hundreds of airplane flights, all of which were connected in some way with business. In no conceivable way was this junket connected with anything but monkey business.

What on earth was I doing? Seventy-five years old, and soaring over the Rocky Mountains for no other reason than to visit a lady whom I had not seen in several years. A postage stamp costs little, but airline travel requires considerable cash. Was I behaving prudently, or was this another of my rash deeds? Had I really prayed about it?

I was on a sentimental journey, gray hairs, hearing aid and all, and was very glad no one on the plane knew me. I thought of Lord Byron as Thomas Wolfe described him, "carrying the pageant of his bleeding heart through Europe." I thought of the great lovers of history, Troilus and Cressida, Antony and Cleopatra, Tristan and Isolde, Abelard and Heloise, all of them tragic figures. And I thought of the fictional Don Quixote on his dilapidated nag Rosinante, singing the glories of a peasant girl whom his imagination turned into Lady Dulcinea del Toboso.

So here I was, "Don" Sherwood in a coach seat on Delta Airlines, buzzing off to meet my 61-year-old friend whom I hadn't seen in years, whom I deeply admired, but about whom I could not think clearly beyond that she was a Christian, a Canadian, was nice, and was unattached.

Now, it's one thing to write "love" at the end of a letter, and quite another thing to kiss someone—I don't mean peck—when all the preliminaries have been paperwork. This was a prospect that occupied a great deal of my attention on that flight and during the change of planes in Minneapolis. After a brief wait I continued on to Winnipeg, arriving just before dark in freezing weather.

As I made my way through the winding corridors of Winnipeg International Airport, I became less and less calm. The dignity of declining years was being shattered. We passengers were herded into a series of rooms where we cleared immigration and claimed our baggage from the conveyor belt. The last step was customs, and here was a large enclosure walled off from the outside world. I stood in a line which moved almost imperceptibly, and thought again, Is this a mistake? Is it another of life's disappointments (of which I had known a few)? Am I really in the center of God's will? Or is this trip for nothing?

A door momentarily opened to the next room, and a large, milling crowd of people came into view. I caught a glimpse of a smile, a waving arm, and a blue coat. Then the door closed, and I continued in line. At last my suitcase was cleared and I was free to go. Again the door opened and I walked into a room full of people moving about, laughing, talking and hugging as the travelers from America were welcomed by those who had been waiting.

I set down my suitcase and looked up. Two boots under a blue coat were advancing toward me.

—

The Red River of the North had leaped its banks, and has been overflowing ever since. Our wedding took place in August, 1987.

Suggestions for Further Reading

James Whitcomb Brougher, Sr., *Life and Laughter,* Valley Forge, Judson Press, 1950.

Donald E. Demaray, *Laughter, Joy and Healing,* Grand Rapids, Baker, 1986.

David Jeremiah, *Turning Toward Joy,* Wheaton IL, Victor Books, 1992.

C. S. Lewis, *Surprised by Joy,* Orlando, FL, Harcourt, Brace, 1956.

William Morrice, *Joy in the New Testament,* Grand Rapids, Eerdmans, 1985.

Cal Samra, *The Joyful Christ,* San Francisco, Harper & Row, 1985.

Charles Swindoll, *Laugh Again,* Dallas, Word Books, 1992.

D. Elton Trueblood, *The Humor of Christ,* San Francisco, Harper & Row, 1964.

Sherwood E. Wirt, *Jesus, Man of Joy,* Nashville, Thomas Nelson, 1991.

Index

D

E

F

K

L

M

N

O

P

R

S

T

U

V

W

Z

About the Author

Sherwood Eliot Wirt is a journalist and author, a retired Presbyterian (USA) minister, and the editor emeritus of *Decision* magazine. He is the author of 25 books, including *Jesus, Man of Joy,* of which 220,000 copies are currently in print. He also edited the Christian Heritage Classics series for the seventeenth through the twentieth centuries. The founder of the San Diego County Christian Writers' Guild, he is winner of the George Washington medal, Freedoms Foundation of Valley Forge, and is former president of the Evangelical Press Association and the San Diego Gilbert & Sullivan Society. He and his wife, the former Ruth Love, have a son and two grandchildren. They make their home in Poway, California.